ADVANCE REVIEWS

"M.L. has taken the essence of her life questioning and put it into a pleasing, extremely readable form. She takes the suffering she has endured and the answers she has found for humanity and puts it in a form that all of us can understand. Not only that, her answers are good and make sense because she did it herself and you can see that in her and in her life. I highly recommend this book for anyone who is questioning and wanting answers."

      ANN KANE, MA, Psychotherapist

"WHIGO is different from other self-help books in that it doesn't send the message that we are broken people who need to be fixed. Rather, WHIGO encourages understanding and compassion of ourselves as a means to finding peace and happiness in our lives. WHIGO encourages us to see our lives and emotions through a lens of honesty so that we can live contentedly with all the experiences that comes with being fully human. This is a must read book."

      V. GALLEGOS, LCSW

"M.L. lauri's work in WHIGO represents a compassionate and skillful integration of a collection of disciplines, including psychology, mental health nursing, and religion/spirituality. She has brought forth her therapeutic insights in a completely relatable manner, stemming from almost four decades of both personal and professional experience. WHIGO is carefully presented in an easy-to-read fashion, giving the reader a step-by-step process for exploring the concepts of personal fulfillment and happiness. M.L. gives the reader a multitude of opportunities to make personal observations, reflect upon their significance, and arrive at a new understanding of their meaning. I would highly encourage anyone willing to take an honest look inside themselves, to read WHIGO as they move through their experience, and bring with them a compelling partner along their road to greater fulfillment, happiness, and peace."

   M. FONTAINE, Psychiatric/Mental Health RN

"This book begins with the most vital question that most of us have thought of, but never said it out loud: What the hell is going on!? It uncovers the fears of readers, the self-buried secrets we keep, and enables the reader to achieve their realization of their own difficulties. The author's approach to the reader's mind is provocative and directed towards self-exploration. The continuous engagement in the writing, mind-questioning of our own self, is what keeps the reader striving for answers. This book puts light on drowning societal behaviors and expectations and redirects the reader to a lighter perspective using the author's vast life experience, multi-cultural exposure, own self-awakening, and continuous strive to find the secrets to true happiness."

   N. FILIPOVIC, Psychiatric/Mental Health RN

WHAT THE HELL IS GOING ON?

WHAT THE HELL IS GOING ON?

The Question
Our Secrets
Some Answers

M.L. lauri

WHAT THE HELL IS GOING ON?
THE QUESTION · OUR SECRETS · SOME ANSWERS
M.L. lauri

ISBN: 978-1-942545-53-8
Library of Congress Control Number: 2016942229

Copyright © 2016 M.L. lauri
All rights reserved.

No part of this book may be reproduced or transmitted in any form or by any means without the written permission of the publisher, except in the case of brief quotations used in book reviews and critical articles.

Published by Expansion
A Publishing Imprint of Wyatt-MacKenzie

DEDICATION

To the relief of the suffering of all sentient beings.

CONTENTS

ACKNOWLEDGEMENTS   i
PREFACE   iii
INTRODUCTION   1

PART I
THE QUESTION

I Beginning with "THE QUESTION"   15
II Lasting, Stable Happiness   19

PART II
OUR SECRETS

I Introduction   35
II Secret Feelings
    1) We're not alone in our pain and suffering.   41
    2) There's a basic sadness that we all experience as part of our human experience.   44
    3) We all want someone to understand how we truly, completely feel.   47
    4) We all get confused about the world around us.   48
    5) We all feel insecure at times.   50
    6) We all want to be happy.   54
    7) We all can feel complete. We just have to do the work to make it happen.   57
    8) We all want to have someone care about us, to be loved.   58

III Secret Thoughts
- 1) We all think there's something wrong with us, that we're incomplete.   64
- 2) We're programmed at a young age to believe what others say about us is true.   66
- 3) Everyone's inner makeup (hard drive) is programmed differently.   70
- 4) No one knows what's going on inside of us but us.   72
- 5) We're taught we're incomplete and need things outside of ourselves for happiness or to feel complete.   73
- 6) We all worry about what others think.   77
- 7) We believe that if someone cares about us, they'll know how we feel and think without us telling them.   79
- 8) We believe it's possible to find or become our "true self."   80

IV Secret Behaviors
- 1) We all wear a mask to the world at times.   83
- 2) We all wear a mask with ourselves at some level.   90
- 3) We believe people's masks are how and who they really are.   96
- 4) We're all doing the best we can for where we are at the time. We're all just doing what we think we need to do to be okay.   101
- 5) We're all just making choices that we believe will make us happy.   103
- 6) Resisting looking at ourselves will only increase our suffering, not make it go away.   105
- 7) No one can make us think, feel, say, or do anything.   108
- 8) We're in control of what we think, feel, say, and do.   109
- 9) We can't make someone else think, feel, say, do, or be anything.   115

10) We're not responsible for what others think, feel, say, or do.	118
11) Others aren't responsible for what we think, feel, say, or do.	122
12) We can't control what others think of us.	124

PART III
SOME ANSWERS

I Introduction	129
II Beginning with Awareness	139
III Experiencing	154
IV Expression and Letting Go	158
V Changing Thoughts	166
VI An Outline for Aware, In-The-Moment Choices	183
VII Whigo	190

PART IV
ENDING WITH THE QUESTION

Ending with "THE QUESTION"	197

APPENDICES

Appendix I	209
An Outline for Aware, In-The-Moment Choices (Synopsis)	
Appendix II	211
The Prayer of Saint Francis of Assisi	
Appendix III	212
The Eight Verses of Thought Transformation	

REFERENCES	213

ACKNOWLEDGEMENTS

First and foremost, I would like to acknowledge my spiritual teachers who have supported me on my path. Lama Zopa Rinpoche who has supported my work on this book since 1996 and my personal growth since 1989. The late Geshe Lama Konchog and Khensur Lama Lhundrup who were not only supportive of my spiritual path and work but were like fathers to me. Thanks to Geshe Yangste Rinpoche who has been supportive of this work since I began to study with him at Maitripa College. My heartfelt gratitude goes out and remains with my dear friend the late Dr. James Blumenthal who not only supported my spiritual studies at Maitripa College but who pushed me to complete the writing of this book and to get it published.

I am thankful to my great friends who have supported me on this journey. My life-long friends Kae Dee Faubion and Agnes Stigall who listened to me talk about this work for so many years and supported me through the whole process. To my girlfriend sister Jeanette Tzyen who not only gave me the feedback I needed on different parts of this work but also took the time to give me feedback on rewrites. She has been and will continue to be my girlfriend sister. To Diane Pettijohn, my dear friend who has listened to and supported me in this work. I would also like to acknowledge all the many people I have met through my life who have helped me to progress on my own spiritual path and those who have helped me increase my insight into this work. There are so many of you. Last but not the least, to my friends and others who have taken their time to review this book.

Last to Nancy Cleary with Wyatt-MacKenzie who understood the need for this book from our first contact and who has assisted me through the publishing process. She has helped me bring my heart's work to fruition. Thank you, Nancy.

PREFACE

Each of us have become who we are based on our genetics and the messages we received from the important people in our lives, especially those messages we received when we were a child. For most of us our parents are a major influence in our lives, positive or negative, as long as they are alive and even after. Whether we are aware of it or not, they helped create our sense of self and what it is that drives us in our lives, whether that is to be successful, a good person, manipulative, etc. For me this translated into being aware of others suffering from a very young age and to have compassion for others, both teachings from my mother. With her death when I was eleven years old, these teachings translated into a drive to understand my own and others suffering, which led me to my work as a nurse and then a psychotherapist. Because this drive was so strong and I had developed a strong awareness into our human suffering, I was driven to find out how to help us all alleviate our suffering, not just superficially but completely. It is this drive that resulted in my life search for answers and this book.

I tried writing this book for thirty years, letting it go at times for different reasons. Each time I let it go, the need for this book would again arise through conversations with people I met along my path. My main goals for writing this book are to help people understand what causes our confusion and suffering, what we all share as human beings, and how to attain the lasting, stable happiness we all seek through understanding the obstacles to happiness and the path and methods to overcome these obstacles. This is not a sugar coated attempt to puff up our weak egos. It is a straight-forward, to the point, but gentle presentation of our human condition and the misconceptions we have that interfere with our happiness. It is a presentation of the thinking that we are all in this together, that we all suffer from our human condition.

My hope is that this book can set you on a course to relieve your suffering. I am open to and hopeful for your comments about this work. I always have more to learn. So please feel free to contact me with your thoughts at **info@mllauri.org**. I hope you find this book helpful and that you learn to be kind to yourself.

M.L. lauri

INTRODUCTION

In the summer after I turned eleven years old, I left home one evening to meet three of my neighborhood friends to go to a movie. When I got there, two of the girls were mad at me. They didn't say why. They just said mean things and didn't want me to go to the movie. Crying, I ran home to my mother. Confused and hurt, I talked to my mom about why my friends acted this way. I went to bed feeling comforted by my mom's love and thinking that I didn't need those girls; after all, I had my mom.

The next morning, I did what I did every Saturday morning. I watched cartoons with my two-year-old brother and four-year-old sister. After we watched TV for a while my sister came to me and said, "Mommy won't wake up. I'm hungry." I then went to see if Mom would get up to fix us breakfast. She looked asleep, so I bent down to wake her up. I then saw what I thought was blood on her pillow (turns out it was tomato juice she had vomited). Terrified, I yelled for my twenty-year-old brother who was home from college. He came running, but he wasn't able to wake her up. He then told me to take my brother and sister out on the porch, and he called an ambulance. He also called my mom's neighbor friend, Margo, who came to get my brother, sister, and me. While I was on the porch

2 WHAT THE HELL IS GOING ON?

with my brother and sister, the two girls who had been unkind to me the night before went by on a bicycle. When they saw me on the porch they started laughing and yelling mean things at me. The next time I saw them the ambulance was there, and they were quiet when they rode past.

My next memory was being at Margo's house and her telling me my mother had died. This was the point where my world began to fall apart. This was the day I lost the center of my universe, my mom. My mother's death was sudden and without warning. She wasn't sick or fragile. So there I was feeling very scared and unable to understand what was going on. I was beyond feeling confused and hurt. I had no idea how to feel, and my mom wasn't there to help me. I was numb.

The day my mother died, my father was out of town at the National Guard's summer training, and my thirteen-year-old sister was out of town with friends. Even though there was no one at my home, when Margo told me my mother died, I decided to take my brother and sister home. When we left Margo's house with her that day, we were stopped by another neighbor, Jean, who began to argue with Margo. Jean's point was that we should come stay with her. Jean was someone I had heard say unkind things to my mother before. I knew my mother didn't see her as a friend. Her daughter, Kathy, was one of the girls who had been mean to me the night before. Even at eleven, I saw that Jean seemed more interested in being the important one in a bad situation. I thought she was more interested in getting something over on Margo than in how we kids were feeling. I remember looking at her and just walking away with my brother and sister.

After that day, I only remember a few things until I returned to school. The one thing that was strong in my mind, though, was others' unkindness towards me and my mother. I remember my mother's funeral and being angry with some people who were there. I was angry with people I thought had been unkind to her or to me, in particular the two girls who had been mean to me the night before and day that my mother died. After that, I only remember one experience with another neighbor, Pat, and nothing else until I returned to school. Sometime after my mother died, Pat came to my room to see me. When she was talking to me I just lay on my bed and stared at the ceiling. I was remembering how she came to our house and yelled at my mother after my older sister got into a fight with her daughter. I was angry and wondering why this woman was talking to me and was in our home. I had never known my mother to be unkind to anyone. Why would Pat have acted this way towards her? Full of anger and confusion, I began to watch people.

This began my journey to try to understand. My journey led me to not only wonder why someone would hurt someone else, but also to understand myself and the world around me. My mother's death opened my eyes to a world that many children don't see until much later in life. I began with asking the question, "Why do people go out of their way to hurt others?" This question was about wanting to understand why my friends had been unkind to me. Because their unkind behavior happened the evening before and the day that my mother died, this was what made me also want to understand why people had been unkind to her. This book is my effort to share with you what I have seen and the true answers I have found on my journey.

At the age of eleven, when my mother died unexpectedly from some still unknown medical problem, my mother was the center of my universe. She was the person I confided in, my best friend, my protector, my teacher, and the one person who gave me unconditional love. Fortunately, I had a very kind and patient mother (I feel for those people who haven't been so fortunate.). My mother wasn't only kind in her interactions with me and others but in her explanations and teachings to me about the world. I remember when I was four years old and came crying into the house because a neighbor kid was eating the sand in my sandbox. My mother didn't go out and tell the kid to stop but explained to me that he came from a poor family. She said, "Maybe he's hungry." A great sadness fell over me that this kid, who was around my age, was so hungry he was eating sand. I don't remember much else except standing there quietly and listening to my mother with this deep feeling of sadness about how much this kid must be suffering to eat sand. The effect of this experience was so strong that I still remember it. This was my mother's way of teaching me. She didn't criticize others but would explain to me why they may have done what they did, and the suffering they were probably experiencing. This was my mother's greatest teaching, to help me be aware of others' suffering and to not be upset with them, but rather to be sympathetic. Following my mother's unexpected death, she wasn't there to help me understand why people had been unkind to her or to help me deal with the loss of her. Because of what I now know was a learned pattern, it was natural for me to cover my fear with anger. As an eleven-year-old not mature enough to understand and express her feelings well, it was also natural that I put my anger onto others. The main objects of my anger were people I thought had been unkind to my mother or to me.

As I said before, after my mother's death, I remember very little until I returned to school. I thought my mother had died in the middle of the summer. I didn't want to know the date. When I reached adulthood I was surprised to find that my mother died about two weeks before school started. I was overweight before she died, but I wasn't when I went back to school. This is why I had always thought the time period was longer. I began to wonder how I could have lost at least twenty pounds in two weeks, so I asked a close cousin about it. She said, "All you did was lie on your bed and stare at the ceiling." I already knew that I had been in shock at that time, but I hadn't realized until the conversation with my cousin that I had been beyond shock. I was completely overwhelmed. Inside I was screaming, "What the hell is going on?" This is why I lost the two weeks between my mother's death and returning to school.

The adults in my life were also very upset, and I don't remember them giving me comfort. You may think "poor little girl." I look, though, at the path my older sister took, who was thirteen when our mother died. She talked about how she felt and often looked for attention and sympathy. It seems to me that her life has been one of continuing to try to fill the loss of our mother with sympathy from others. In my view this behavior hasn't helped her find much happiness. I turned inside instead, and started asking questions about the world around me. This turning inside, and concentrating on the hurt that I felt from others' unkindness towards myself and my mother, led me to question why some people seem to go out of their way to hurt others. This turned into wanting to understand myself and the world around me. Yes, to this day I would like to have my mother back in my life; *but* would I have set out on this journey of discovery without this overwhelming trauma? Would I have found the lasting, stable happiness that I have now? Maybe yes, maybe no.

I know now that my journey of asking questions and looking for answers is what led to my career in psychology. After years of study and practice in Western psychology systems, I became frustrated because nothing seemed to really talk about the human suffering that I saw. Western psychology seemed to look at identifying people's problems or symptoms of a problem. Little time was given, even in school, to talking about and studying our human condition: the suffering we experience just by being human. Yes, I studied theories of human development, but there was nothing that seemed to really talk about our human condition, our basic human suffering. I couldn't find anything that told me how to help people deal with the everyday pain and suffering that goes with just being alive. It was like people were coming to me for help, and I was only helping them to put on a bandage. How could I really help them with this deeper suffering?

Troubled by my continuing desire to understand human suffering, my own and others', I explored different ideas from the New Age movement and other self-development methods. Along with my wish to understand, I, like all human beings, was looking to find a lasting, stable happiness. I married and discovered it didn't bring this happiness. I wondered if maybe I just hadn't found the right man. Somewhere inside I knew, though, that finding the right man wasn't the answer, although it didn't stop me from looking. I had been the replacement mother for my younger brother and sister after our mother's death. As much as I loved them, I knew from my experience that children weren't the answer to lasting happiness.

Because I wasn't finding answers, I then began to travel. I traveled to the Caribbean, Western Europe, North Africa, Canada, Mexico, and different places in the USA. In many of these places I "partied," which included alcohol, dancing, and gambling. I played at the Spanish, Italian, and French Rivera, even Monaco. I searched the places of romance novels for this happiness, but it continued to escape me.

Because my efforts to find happiness outside of myself through "partying" and traveling weren't successful, leaving me still troubled by a wish for lasting happiness and answers, I continued to explore different New Age and Western self-development methods. I also became involved with The Association for Humanistic Psychology. These self-development opportunities opened me up to an inner path, but they didn't give me the answers I needed to change the negative parts of myself that I didn't want. I somehow understood that my negative parts were getting in the way of my becoming a more loving, more understanding, and happier person. I remember talking about my negative thoughts and feelings with different teachers I met. My main question was about what to do with the anger that came up when I felt someone might harm me. I usually got the answer, "Just send them love." I would reply, "I'm not feeling love. What do I do with this anger and fear?" I never got a satisfactory answer. I knew from my psychology training that just denying how I felt and trying to pretend that I was feeling love wasn't the answer. Discouraged, I decided to take a year off from my work as a psychotherapist to travel. Having already traveled to many places, I wanted to go someplace different. I decided to go next to Asia. Unknown to me at that time, I was about to find the answers I was looking for.

Before I left to travel to Asia I thought I was taking only a year off from my psychotherapist career (I had no idea I would live in Asia for eight years.) Also at that time, one question that continued to bother me was, "If everyone around me is suffering from this basic human condition, how do we really help people?" I'm not referring to depression or grief, but to this basic human suffering that we all seem to experience. Even my co-workers, psychiatrists, psychologists, social workers, nurses, and so on, all of these mental health professionals (who probably know more than the average person about helping others deal with suffering) had this basic human suffering. Some were trying to face their suffering head on. Others hid from it, while others tried to distract themselves from it with drugs, sex, or good old rock and roll.

After my mother's death I was left with much of the care of my younger brother and sister and with keeping the house. My father brought in the money and did the cooking, but I did most of the housework and was the emotional support for the family. Because of this situation,

I never had the energy to keep up any pretenses. I have never been what American teenagers call a "poser," "pretender," or "wanna be." This type of person is someone who is pretending to think, feel, or be other than what they are. Instead I have always been what Americans call a bottom-line person. So here I was, wondering what the bottom line was with this human suffering we all have; bottom line, how is it possible to help people reduce their suffering? To find the answers I took a year off and headed for Asia.

My travels in Asia began in the summer of 1988. As I traveled I began to wonder, "Is basic human suffering different from culture to culture?" The Western people I met and enjoyed the most were students of Buddhism. There also seemed to be some difference in the outlook of the Asian Buddhist people I met. It isn't good to generalize too much, but many of them seemed more peaceful and more in touch with their kindness. These experiences made me want to explore what Buddhism was all about.

On my trip to Kathmandu, Nepal, I decided to attend a course on Buddhism at Kopan Monastery. Much to my surprise, at the course they talked directly about the very questions that were troubling me. "What is this basic human suffering we all experience?" "How do we really help ourselves and others deal with this basic human suffering?" They also had an answer to my question about what to do with the anger or fear that I felt any time I thought I might be harmed. I began to understand that basic human suffering is just that: *basic human* suffering. Human suffering doesn't differ from culture to culture because human beings are human beings no matter what their culture. This course was the start of my ongoing journey of using Buddhist ideas for my self-development and in my search to help others decrease their suffering. I had found my bottom line. I found the philosophy and methods that could not only help me to develop myself but could also help me to help others. I found a way of thinking that directly deals with our basic human condition, our suffering.

This book is an effort to provide the information I have come to know and understand over the years. My hope is that this information can help to increase your happiness and decrease your suffering. What I am presenting isn't complicated, and hopefully I have been skillful enough to write this book in a way that's easy to understand. I'm not saying that I have all the answers; in fact, I have told many clients that if your therapist tells you *your* answers, run away. Only you can come up with your answers. As I do with clients, I only hope to give you some ways to help yourself and to give you some facts that I have come to know. My hope is that this information will help you avoid spending a lot of years looking for answers. Some of what I have written here I hold as factual, some as opinion. When I believe something to be a fact I will say so; but remember you always have the choice to believe or not believe what I say. If you want to find a more stable, lasting happiness, the very first step is to begin to think for yourself. In other words, the first step is to look at and think about what you have been and are being told, so that you can decide if *you* believe these things to be true or not.

I first began thinking about writing this book in 1986 when I was working as a psychotherapist in an outpatient clinic. One day I went into a staff meeting and told my co-workers I was going to write a book called "What the hell is going on?" because that was the question I heard asked all day long. We all laughed. They thought I was joking, but part of me knew I was serious. Over the years, I came to understand that I had to work on improving myself more (so that I could "walk what I talked") if I was going to be able to provide the information in a true way. So over the next thirty years I talked about this book, wrote some, worked on myself, watched others, questioned, talked some more, and watched some more. Every time I put this book aside, thinking that I wasn't able to write it, or that it wasn't really needed, I would find myself in a conversation about the ideas in this book. It was interesting where these conversations would come up. It wasn't just with friends. Most of these conversations were with strangers whom I met on a plane or while waiting somewhere for something and so forth. The need for this book always seemed to come back to me, whether I was in America, in Asia, or on my way somewhere, everywhere.

The book begins with "the question," then discusses the secrets of our shared human experiences. I call them "secrets" because it seems that many of us are unaware of these experiences, or if we are aware, we don't talk openly about them, so they are like secrets. Following these sections is the answers section. This section is where we talk about how we can begin a journey to find our specific answers. The information in this book can function as a beginning structure to help decrease our suffering and increase our happiness.

Often, as I write, I will refer to "we" versus "I." This is to give credit to all those wise people who have helped me on my way and to help us remember that this author is also human and continues to struggle along with you. The answers I am presenting here have helped make my struggle much easier. Also, this book isn't about Buddhist thinking; however, I believe that Buddhism would agree with most of what I have to say. It also isn't an effort to try to get anyone to think any certain way. In fact, it was my Christian beliefs that helped me deal with the death of my mother. It has been the Buddhist beliefs that have helped to strengthen my own thinking and have helped with my inner, personal development. I can't say enough that only you can decide which ways can help you with whatever goals you have. My goal is to help you begin or progress on your journey to a more lasting, stable happiness. With this in mind, I end the book by returning back to "the question," by sharing with you some of the specific answers I have found to my personal questions, and by sharing my hope for all of our futures.

· PART ONE ·
THE QUESTION

I

Beginning with "THE QUESTION"

Remember when I talked about how I was screaming, "What the hell is going on?" after my mother died? This was a traumatic situation that caused me to ask this question, but can you see that I was also asking the question when my friends were unkind to me? I've often had clients in my office crying and trying to figure out why someone did something or why something happened. They were all asking, "What the hell is going on?"

We usually go about our day pretty happy until something doesn't go the way we want. Maybe the alarm clock doesn't go off, or something worse happens like what happened to me: you lose someone. As long as events in our life are going along smoothly like we want, we smile and feel easy with the world around us. This doesn't mean that we aren't suffering. It only means that we usually aren't asking questions at these times. After all, why question a good thing? When something interferes with what we want, which is often, at least on a small scale, we get upset. When the interference is small, we might ask, "What's going on?" and just feel irritated, even though we might not be aware of our irritation. As the size of the interference increases, though, our emotions become stronger and everything around us seems more of a problem. The biggest interference seems to come from our relationships with others. As our unpleasant emotions increase, our happiness seems more disrupted. This is when the question changes from "What is going on?" to "What the hell is going on?" Cussing or profanity just seems to help express the intensity of our unpleasant feelings and unhappiness. This is the reason the question in this book is, "What the hell is going on?" We aren't really talking about the small interruptions to our happiness. We are talking about the bigger interruptions, the ones that have a greater effect on our happiness.

This book is about looking at and talking about our basic human suffering, how we can decrease it and how we can increase our happiness. We're talking about the question "What the hell is going on?" because it's the question my clients ask over and over. I've also heard this question from many other people. In fact, I recently heard this question asked on two different news shows on TV. Of course, they said, "What the heck is going on?" and, "What the devil is going on?" If you start to pay attention you'll notice, like I did, that this is a question people ask a lot. I often joke and say I think it must be the most frequently-asked question on the planet.

The question that usually comes after "What the hell is going on?" is "Why?" No one can answer "Why?" about every situation that occurs, but as we better understand ourselves and what we have in common with others we can gain some understanding about why some things might happen. The only way we can really know why someone did something is to ask them. Even then, our understanding is going to depend on how honest the person is willing to be. The greatest problem we really have with understanding anything is more about the thinking patterns we've developed over the years. It's this way of thinking that we use to understand what happens around us; and this thinking affects our own ability to understand the thinking and choices of others.

As far as the things that happen in the universe, who can answer these questions? Some people turn to religion for answers, some to science. Some use a combination of the two. I'm not trying to explain the universe here; I'm just trying to increase our understanding of our human condition, our basic human suffering. Hopefully this understanding and the answers in section three will help us reduce our suffering and increase our happiness.

If we understand and live in a way that makes a lasting happiness, we'll find that the question "What the hell is going on?" will come up, but it will be more like "whigo?" Whigo (pronounced whig-oe) is the acronym for "What the hell is going on?" Say whigo out loud. Whigo is a word that seems to make us smile. It has a more positive feeling to it, and it's hard to say with anger or confusion. There will always be situations that come up that we don't understand. We'll never understand why *all* people do what they do or why some events happen in nature, but if we learn to approach our inability to understand with whigo? then our happiness isn't so affected. Our happiness is more stable because we're not caught up in trying to understand things we aren't able to understand. Our confusion gets reduced because we can smile and understand that we can't know all the answers. We smile, say "whigo?" and let the confusion go, because there are just some things we will never understand.

Whether we're feeling anger, fear, or some other unpleasant emotion when we're asking "What the hell is going on?" or "Why?", confusion is the one feeling that's there in all of us. Can we keep a lasting and stable happiness when we're full of confusion? We'll talk about this next.

II

Lasting, Stable Happiness

Once I was in a class on Buddhism in north India. There was a man there who said he was American, and that he left America because people lied to him about how to find happiness. He said he next went to Australia looking for happiness and was now very angry because "they lied to me, too." Most people aren't really aware that a large part of who we become is the result of the culture or the society where we grow up. If our culture or society tells us there is happiness in a family or a house and two cars, we'll try to get these because, after all, we all want happiness. If we get these things, and we're still not happy, then we get confused or angry and ask, "What the hell is going on? Did someone lie to me? Do I just have the wrong wife/husband, wrong house or wrong job? Am I just in the wrong country?" We then try to change something, so we can be happy again. *"What the hell is going on here?!"* Can the answer to lasting happiness really be found in a new house, new job, or new wife/husband/partner, or by moving to a different country? How do we find the happiness we're looking for and keep it?

There's a television commercial I saw several years ago that was done by a religious group. It showed a small boy sitting on the stairs in his house, crying. His mother then came up and yelled at him. The commercial then showed the boy sitting on the stairs again, crying. This time his mother came up, put her arms around him, and asked him what was wrong. Words then came on the screen saying something like, "Your children are what you tell them they are." From my experience of working with people and myself I have found this to be true. When we're born, our parents and the people around us teach us how to walk and talk and a lot more. One of the biggest mistakes that parents make is to judge and make statements about their child's behavior without separating the behavior from the child's identity, who the child is. There's a big difference between telling a child that their behavior is bad versus telling them they are bad. This book isn't about parenting, though. Parenting has been brought up to show how we develop what we think about ourselves. How we think about ourselves, our self-esteem or our judgments about ourselves, is very important because our self-esteem has a very strong effect on how we see and experience the world.

Research on genes (DNA) shows that our genes do play a part in who we are or who we become. There's no doubt that part of what we are comes from our genes. At a minimum our genes create the color of our skin, our hair, and our eyes, and the organs that we need for our body to live and function. I doubt we could find a researcher, though, who would say for sure that all we are or have become is totally because of our genes. This is because we can't rule out the effect of experience on each of us.

When I talk about who we are, our inner make-up, I like to use a comparison between us and a computer. Whether the computer is a desk top, lap top, or our smart phone, it is made up of its outer case, the hard drive that holds the basic programs so that it can function, and software programs (or apps) that we have put on it. Our brain is like the hard drive of a computer, the computer being our body and brain. When you buy a new computer (our birth) there is some programming already in place on the hard drive. These are the basic programs, the operating system, that allow the computer to work. With us, we can compare these programs on our hard drive (brain) to our genes. Our genes give us our operating system in the form of our body functions. We then go on to add new things, software programs, to our hard drive. These software programs are made up of the experiences we have in our lives. So part of what we'll look at here is whether we want to continue to get up each morning, reboot our computer (ourselves), and just run on our often hidden, software programs, *or* do we want to start to look at the software programs that were placed on our hard drive over the years? Do we want to begin to question what software (much of which is unknown to us) has been placed on our hard drive? In other words, do we want to begin to question and look at what experiences have been kept in our brain in the form of aware and unaware memories (software programs)? Are we ready to begin to think for ourselves? This last question isn't meant to be offensive. It's meant to start us thinking about whether our thoughts, feelings, and choices come from aware, in-the-moment, present-day decisions. If not, then they are from automatic thought-feeling patterns that are part of software programs (life experiences put on our hard drive in the form of memories) that come up automatically in situations without us being aware of thinking about things. They can seem like habits.

Remember how I said that the anger I felt when my mother died was from a learned pattern? Later in life I saw that in my family it was okay to be angry but not afraid. Remember Kathy, one of the girls who was mean to me the night before my mother died? Many years later when we were in our thirties, I got together with a bunch of the girls I grew up with. Kathy was there. At one point Kathy and another woman started talking with me about the day my mother died, and how I was after. Kathy said, "You were always so angry." I said, "I was terrified. My world fell apart. My family doesn't get scared, they get angry." Kathy and the other woman both understood. They both knew this was how my family was, not necessarily an angry family, but a family that presented itself as proud and very strong. In my family, showing fear wouldn't be acting strong or proud. The program that my family helped to create in me was that when you're afraid, be strong. Anger is strong. Right? So anger became part of a pattern in my self-defense program. When you're afraid, stand strong and show anger if necessary.

LET'S STOP FOR A MINUTE. Let's think about this.
I learned a pattern of how to react in a situation when I was feeling threatened. Do you think this pattern in my self-defense program was put there on purpose by my family, or did I learn this pattern some other way? **Stop now and think. WHIGO?** *Do you think my responding*

to others with anger made me happy? **But** *what about you? Are you aware of what you were taught about how to respond when you feel threatened? Does this response help you or cause you suffering?*

Unfortunately, it's not so easy to get rid of these programs in our brain (memories, learned behavior, automatic thought-feeling patterns, habits) that we don't like, but it is possible to get rid of how strong they are. We'll talk about this in the answers chapter, how to decrease the strength of the programs in our brain that cause us suffering. In other words, the answers tell us how we can decrease our suffering, increase our happiness, and gain a lasting, stable happiness. We enter into the chapter about secrets first because there's so much about our shared human experiences that people don't seem to know. This doesn't say anything about who we are. If we don't know about these experiences, it only means that, for whatever reason, we just didn't look. Increasing our understanding of our shared human condition helps us find happiness because it decreases our feelings of being alone and isolated. Decreasing these feelings helps to create the higher self-esteem we need for a lasting, stable happiness.

One of the major things that keeps us from getting the lasting, stable happiness we all want is a false myth that most societies in the world believe is true. This false myth is that we can find a lasting, stable happiness through getting things outside of ourselves, through finding the right person, making a lot of money, accomplishing certain things, obtaining objects and the list goes on and on. Most societies say and believe that this myth is true, so this search for happiness outside of ourselves is how people learn to look for happiness; believing in this false myth drives people to make money so that they can get the outside objects they need to be happy. Because we're taught that this myth is true, it becomes a strong part of the belief system that we use to interact with the world (it becomes a software program on our hard drive). I say that it's a fact that this myth is false. It is a mistaken belief. I base my thinking on my research, observations, and personal journey to try to understand our common human suffering and to find a way to decrease this suffering. Most important, though, I found the true way to gain the lasting, stable happiness that all people search for. I found the answers. A lasting happiness cannot be found outside of ourselves; it must be found from within.

There's a woman I know who was so excited and happy when she was able to buy her first new car. Later I remember her calling when someone had scratched it. She was very upset. After that, every time she saw the scratch on her new car she felt sad. Her car had moved from causing her happiness to causing her unhappiness. We all know someone who was so happy when they got married and so unhappy when they got divorced. The relationship that had created so much happiness in the person changed to cause them suffering. These are examples of looking outside of ourselves for happiness that worked for a short time, but then ended up the cause of so much unhappiness. The happiness didn't last.

LET'S STOP FOR A MINUTE. Let's think about this. *Have you ever known someone who was so happy about something they got or accomplished and later was so un-*

happy about it? Have you ever known someone who found a lasting, stable happiness with outside things? **Stop now and think. WHIGO?** *We can think about others' experiences,* **but** *what about your experiences? Have you ever been happy in a relationship and then later unhappy in the same relationship? Have you ever gotten something that made you happy and later felt unhappy when it broke, tore up, or simply got too old to use? Did your search for happiness with these outside things get you the lasting, stable happiness you wanted, or did you end up confused, frustrated, or unhappy?*

There are many famous people we can look at who seemed to have all the outside objects, accomplishments and relationships we would need to be happy, yet they were unhappy. Princess Diana was one of them. She had wealth, fame, beauty, and healthy children, yet she openly shared with us that she wasn't happy. Now she didn't have a positive partner in her life, but we have already talked about how relationships can be a source of happiness that goes away, which was certainly the case for Princess Diana.

Most societies believe that the false myth is true, so they encourage people to seek outside things (objects, people, accomplishments, and so on), so that they can be happy or feel better in some way. This false myth, though, is really an exaggerated reality, a reality based on mistaken beliefs. It's just not true that collecting objects, people, and accomplishments will help us reach our main goal of a lasting, stable happiness. In fact, this outside search for happiness causes unhappiness and suffering simply because the happiness it brings goes away. We are then once again unhappy and confused.

The false myth also encourages the false belief that outer things, people, events, and so on, are responsible for our feelings, thoughts, and behavior. Blaming outside things for what we think, feel, or do leads to a feeling of helplessness. This helplessness stops us from developing self-confidence or high self-esteem. We can't be successful in getting a lasting, stable happiness if we're feeling insecure and have low self-esteem. If we understand that this belief is false we can then follow a way that helps us to reduce our suffering. Taking responsibility for our thoughts, feelings, and behaviors ends this feeling of helplessness. It lets us create the inner strength, confidence, and positive self-esteem we need for a lasting, stable happiness. If we understand that lasting happiness and a positive self-esteem can only be found by looking inside ourselves, we have the way to find and keep the lasting happiness and confidence we seek.

While I was living in India, I often asked different Indians I knew if they were happy. Most of these people were poor. They all said, "I've never thought about it." When I thought about what they said, I often thought about a famous, American psychologist named Abraham Maslow, who has a theory about how we develop based on our needs.

Maslow created a pyramid he called *Maslow's Hierarchy of Needs* that he used to explain how we move through different levels of needs until we reach the top of his pyramid. He says we don't move from one level to the next until we meet the needs of the level that we're on (Maslow, 1943). At the bottom of his pyramid are our most basic needs for food, water, and shelter. We then move up his pyramid, completing our needs for safety, the "needs for love, affection, and belongingness," and the "need for self-esteem," until we reach the top of his pyramid, which is the need for "self-actualization" (Maslow, 1943). The Merriam-Webster dictionary defines self-actualization as "to realize fully one's potential" (Merriam-Webster 2011 edition). In this book, we're talking about realizing our full potential for happiness, our self-actualization of happiness. What is it that keeps us from finding or reaching our full potential for happiness? Can we reach our full potential for happiness outside of ourselves? Were my Indian friends not thinking about being happy because they were caught up in getting their basic needs met?

Before answering these questions, let's talk about how our societies reinforce the false myth that happiness can be found outside of us. How many people are really aware that their goals of wealth, fame, prestige, and so forth, all those outer things that people seem to want, won't really help them find and keep a lasting happiness? I think not many. I think the people in a society who encourage this false belief, especially the false idea that money can bring happiness, are also victims of this false myth. Being humans that have also grown up with this myth, they, like most of us, continue to live and believe in the false myth in hopes of reaching their goals. Most aren't really aware that it's not true that we can find a lasting happiness outside of ourselves.

LET'S STOP FOR A MINUTE. Let's think about this.
If our society teaches us that we can find happiness outside of ourselves with objects, people, and accomplishments, why wouldn't we believe this is true? If we look to these outside things for happiness and it doesn't work,

> *how do we feel about ourselves? If we blame others for how we think, feel or behave, how is it that we feel helpless?* **Stop now and think. WHIGO?** *Is high self-esteem and confidence really necessary for people to find lasting happiness?* **But** *what about you? How do you feel when the outside things you are looking to for happiness don't bring you a lasting happiness? Does this lack of success affect your self-esteem? How do you feel when you blame others for what you are thinking, feeling, or doing? Does this help you feel strong and increase your self-esteem or cause some kind of suffering?*

If we look at human history, it's easy to see how the false myth came about. When our ancestors were without any modern comforts, it's understandable that finding food, water, warmth, and shelter, and the company of others was a way to get happiness. This is because these outside things were necessary for their well-being. Getting these outer things obviously contributed to their happiness and well-being. If a lasting happiness can be found with outside things, though, why haven't we been successful in finding and keeping it? For those of us whose basic needs of food, water, and shelter have been met, why is it that our search for happiness continues to be outside?

The false myth, and the false belief, that things outside of us are responsible for how we think, feel, or behave, cause a feeling of helplessness that interferes with our development of a positive self-esteem. We have already talked about how the myth causes this helplessness through encouraging the false belief. The myth also causes a feeling of helplessness because when our repeated, outside attempts to find a lasting happiness aren't successful, we are then left feeling even more confused, and thereby helpless, about how to find this lasting happiness we seek. The false belief causes helplessness because if others are responsible for how we think, feel, or behave, then this means that somehow they must be in control of us. They decide how we are going to think, feel, or behave; otherwise, it just can't be true that they are responsible for our choices. If they're in control of us then we're helpless to do or choose any other way to think, feel, or behave. Because of this, Maslow's theory would say that it's not possible to achieve our full potential for happiness if we believe in this myth and false belief. Maslow says that when the need for self-esteem isn't met, then "the person feels inferior, weak, helpless and worthless" (Maslow, 1943).

In many societies there are advertising firms who hire psychology professionals to figure out how to make us want to buy their products. They do this because they believe they can influence us by getting at our insecurities or vulnerabilities. The heart of our insecurities and vulnerabilities, though, lies in this false myth that says we can find and keep a lasting happiness from things outside of ourselves. It seems that Maslow and I both believe that without creating a positive self-esteem, a sense of positive self-value, we can't really reach our full potential for happiness: a lasting, stable happiness. Only through creating a positive sense of self can we find and keep a lasting, stable happiness.

As long as we continue an outer search for happiness we will be caught up in an ongoing loop that not only causes a feeling of helplessness but prevents us from achieving a healthy, positive self-esteem. This loop begins with our believing that we can find happiness by getting outside things. Because this method won't be successful, it creates a sense of helplessness and unhappiness along with low self-esteem. We then try again to get rid of our unhappiness by looking for happiness in the way we believe it can be found, outside of us through objects, people, etc. Once again this outside search won't be successful, and we will feel unhappy and helpless. This carries on and completes the loop. We go around and around, but a lasting, stable happiness continues to escape us.

So to state things clearly, I believe that the root of our problems (and thereby the world's problems) comes from believing we can find happiness outside of ourselves through getting objects, collecting people, accomplishments, power, praise, and on and on. Believing that this is the way to successfully get lasting happiness, we put a lot of energy into getting these outside things. What it is that we have been taught, and believe, will bring us lasting happiness is what will determine how we will try to get this happiness. After all, what we all seek is happiness. It's the main thing that causes us to do most of what we do. When we get these outside things and still don't have the lasting happiness we want, confusion often arises. Only through knowing the root of our confusion can we find and keep the lasting happiness we are looking for.

There are many examples of how looking to outer things for lasting happiness doesn't work. We can see many people who have all the outer things that one might desire such as fame, prestige, money, beauty, family, success, and so forth. People like Princess Diana, Kurt Cobain, Heath Ledger, Robin Williams, and Whitney Houston are good examples. These were people who had all the outer things one might think would help them keep a lasting happiness, yet they used drugs, committed suicide, or simply allowed us to see their pain and suffering. There's a TV show on now called *Million Dollar American Princesses* that tells the life stories of many millionaire, American women. Most of their stories are about an unhappy life. They had every outside thing that we would think we would need to be happy, but they weren't.

There are two false beliefs that cause our confusion and interfere with finding and keeping a lasting happiness. These two roots of our confusion are what create the question, "What the hell is going on?" The first one we have just discussed: believing in the false myth that we can be successful in finding happiness through things outside of ourselves. The other we have touched on briefly: the feeling of being alone in our human condition.

If we go back to Maslow's theory, we can see that we can't develop positive self-esteem without first meeting our needs for love, affection, and belonging. Can these needs really be met if we believe we are alone in our human condition and the feelings and thoughts that are part of this condition? I say no. I say this feeling of being alone in our human experience creates a feeling of isolation. It's the opposite of the feeling of belonging that Maslow says we must achieve in order to be able to move on to the next level, meeting our self-esteem needs.

The purpose of this book is to show two ways these false beliefs cause us confusion and interfere with our ability to find a lasting, stable happiness. I'm showing the first way by openly talking about our shared human experiences (in Section II called "Our Secrets") with the hope of decreasing our feelings of being alone and isolated. If our feelings of being alone and isolated are decreased, then our needs for love, affection, and belonging can be achieved or strengthened. Achieving or strengthening these needs will then help us achieve the positive self-esteem that we need for lasting happiness. The second way is through making us aware that some inside path (discussed in Section III as "Some Answers "), whatever we may choose that to be, is the main way to get the lasting, stable happiness we want. Until we understand these two things we aren't going to find the answers to the question, "What the hell is going on?" or be able to keep the lasting, stable happiness we seek.

Once we do begin to understand and live in a way that supports a lasting, stable happiness, we will find that the question "What the hell is going on?" may come up, but we will be experiencing it more like whigo? As I said before, situations will come up in life that we don't understand, but we'll no longer respond with confusion; rather, we'll respond with whigo? Approaching the world and the situations that come up with whigo? and a smile helps us keep a stable happiness. Also, as we begin to understand these ideas, our relationship with outside objects and people will change, and we will begin to experience the interesting side effect of enjoying our relationships and outside objects much more than we did when we were looking to them for happiness. This is because once we no longer look to outside things for happiness, this lack of expectations allows us to enjoy them more than we ever had. It's like an extra, special bonus.

· PART TWO ·
OUR SECRETS

I

Introduction

One day I had a new client come to my office. When he walked in I saw a handsome, healthy, young man dressed in a nice suit. To look at him, no one would think he might have any problems. As I started to learn about his life it seemed that he was successful in his job, had several friends, and his family was supportive. As we continued to talk he shared that he didn't feel that he really had anyone in his life. He felt totally alone, and this feeling of being totally alone was making him feel more and more depressed.

> **LET'S STOP FOR A MINUTE. Let's think about this.** *Here was a man who seemed to have everything we might want to be happy, but he wasn't.* **Stop now and think. WHIGO?** *Think about what he might be feeling,* ***but*** *what about you? Have you ever known someone who you thought was happy and had no problems only to find out later that they did?*

Psychotherapists learn quickly that people share many secrets with them that they hide from others. Even though I'd worked in the field of psychology for five years before I became a psychotherapist, it wasn't until I started my psychotherapist job that I started to understand just how much we all hide ourselves from others. This hiding is usually about feeling vulnerable or concerned about what others might think about us. It's certainly about our self-esteem. When I was a new psychotherapist I was often surprised when someone, who outwardly appeared to "have it all together" (successful in their profession, attractive, and had many friends), shared with me just how alone, sad, insecure, or scared they really were.

As I watched and became more aware of the signs of people's low self-esteem, I also became aware that low self-esteem was something many of us have in common; it's part of our human condition. I'm still often surprised, though, by how unaware people are of our common human experiences. In my years of working in mental health and searching for answers, I had come to take for granted many of these observations, seeing them as common sense about people, relationships, and our human makeup. At some point in my searching, I realized that these were common sense to me because I've been looking at and helping others to understand these experiences for many years, so naturally I'm very aware of them. I started calling these common human experiences "secrets" because I found that even if we superficially know that other people might have these feelings or experiences, we often keep our own to ourselves, secret, for many reasons.

When I talk about these secrets I often use the nouns "everyone" or "we all" because I'm talking about a large part of the human population. Those who already understand and are comfortable with these secrets have greatly decreased their suffering. Most of them will admit, though, that there was a time when they also weren't aware of these secrets. I'm not talking here about superficial awareness. I'm talking about a true knowing awareness. Some of these secrets may seem simple and even common sense, but over the years I have met people from all over the world, from different religions, cultures, and walks of life who weren't aware of these secrets. Of course if we ask some of these people if they're aware of these secrets, they might reply, "Of course!" If we investigate, though, we'll often find that although they may have some intellectual understanding that these are truths, they don't necessarily know them well enough to live them. They're also probably not comfortable with sharing that they have these experiences themselves. For many of us, to admit we experience these secrets is to make ourselves vulnerable. This is why I'm talking about them here. I want to remove the false belief that anyone *never* experiences these secrets.

The most surprising group I've found that seems to be unaware of these common human experiences (secrets) is some of the Buddhist practitioners whom I've met. I found, and I continue to find, this surprising because as I have said before, Buddhism directly addresses our basic human suffering. We would think that if someone studies Buddhism they would automatically become aware of these secrets; but from my experience that doesn't seem to be the case. This lack of awareness is because, as I said before, it's one thing to have an intellectual understanding about something, but it's different to have it as part of our inner understanding. This lack of awareness seems to be more common with Western practitioners than with those born into an Asian Buddhist family. This is probably because a child born into an Asian Buddhist family is likely to grow up with these understandings. These understandings are part of the software programs that are put on their hard drive as they grow up. It's part of their culture. This software, though, isn't put on the hard drive of most Western Buddhists as they're growing up. For most Westerners, it's a chosen software program they add to their hard drive when they're older. Of course, even Westerners born into a Buddhist family often have these ideas as part of their software programs, so they are likely to have more awareness of these common human sufferings.

Once I was waiting in line at a doctor's office in Nepal. At that time, I had studied Buddhism for several years and had been a psychotherapist for many more years. I was sitting next to a young Tibetan (Buddhist) man. At one point a well-dressed Nepali man walked past and cut to the front of the line. I became angry and said to the young man, "What's wrong with him? Who does he think he is?" The young man, who was much younger than I, seemed sad and started talking about the suffering this man must have experienced in order to act this way. As I listened to him talk, I felt ashamed. My first reaction was a selfish, unaware reaction. His was one of compassion and concern for the man, a quite different reaction. This situation helped me to begin to understand that I had developed an intellectual understanding of the wisdom in the Buddhist thinking, but had not taken these wise teachings into an inner, heart understanding, an understanding that I could live and put into practice. A Tibetan man I worked with told me that Tibetan children are taught to think of others first; it is part of their culture. This teaching is why the young Tibetan man thought first of the feelings of the man before himself. It has taken me time to learn to react this way and make the Buddhist wisdom part of how I live and interact with others, to make it an inner, heart software program.

Because my hope is to decrease our suffering, I start the list of secrets by talking about the most basic secret, "We're not alone in our pain and suffering." It's important to understand that we all experience suffering. I believe all the secrets are factual characteristics of our human suffering, not just my opinion. Each secret is explained in this book, but several aren't explained in depth. Instead, I have chosen to talk more about some of them in the answers chapter to show how they can be used to decrease our suffering and increase our happiness. The secrets are separated into secret feelings, thoughts, and behavior, but they really overlap with each other. They have been separated in this way to make them easy to explain and understand.

The only people I have found who might not experience some of these secrets are those who are usually called sociopaths. As we go through these secrets, if we don't believe we experience one of them, it doesn't mean we're a sociopath. A sociopath probably wouldn't read this book. If we believe we haven't had one of these experiences, it's probably because we haven't looked at or watched our experiences in some way in order to be aware that we've had these experiences. It says nothing more about us than this. Now maybe, what I'm saying isn't true. *Remember*, it's important that we check for ourselves to see if we believe that what's being talked about is true. Just because I've said it, doesn't mean anyone should blindly believe it. Watch. Pay attention to yourself and others. Don't allow what I say to be another unexamined software program on your hard drive.

II

Secret Feelings

1) We're not alone in our pain and suffering.

In the summer of 1988, I was in a small village in China called Yangzhou. One day I was waiting at the side of the road for a friend, and an old Chinese woman came walking by. The look on her face seemed angry. She seemed to be unhappy and suffering. I looked at her and said "Ni Hao," which is "Hi" in Chinese. She then totally changed. She began smiling and patting me saying, "Ni Hao, Ni Hao." I don't know if she was happy because a foreigner said hello to her in her own language or what, but for a brief moment, the suffering on her face changed to joy. It doesn't matter if we are American, African, or Chinese. *Everyone* experiences suffering. I have often thought about this situation and wondered how lovely it would be if I could bring joy to others just by saying "Hello." I take that chance now and always greet anyone who crosses my path.

LET'S STOP FOR A MINUTE. **Let's think about this**.
Everyone experiences suffering. Think about this. Is it possible that religious leaders, famous people, or world

leaders experience suffering? **Stop now and think. WHIGO?** *Do you think everyone experiences suffering? But what about you? Have you ever met anyone who you thought had never suffered? Do you think that a person responding to you in a negative way is suffering?*

You say, "Of course I know that others feel pain and suffering." I wonder, though, just how aware we really are that others feel pain and suffering. When we're interacting with another person, are we aware of their suffering, especially if the interaction is negative? For example, why do you think so many people like American television talk shows like Jerry Springer or Dr. Phil? Is it just about being entertained? I don't think so. It's mainly because the people on these shows share their pain and suffering. Watching these shows helps us feel like we're not alone in our suffering. Sometimes watching these shows may make us feel superior to others or better about ourselves. Why is this? This is because it's a superficial, temporary way of increasing our self-esteem. Why do we buy magazines with information about celebrities and the problems they're having? We buy them because it helps us to feel better because we're not alone in having problems or in our suffering. After all, if someone so famous, who has so much, has problems, maybe our pain and suffering isn't so much. The bottom line is that we get comfort from knowing that we're not alone in our pain and suffering. Knowing we're not alone in our pain and suffering is very important to remember because when we're caught up in our own pain and suffering, we tend to feel very much alone. It's times like these when the feeling of being alone in our suffering becomes the strongest. Maybe you say, "Who cares?

Remembering that others have pain and suffering doesn't help me." But this isn't true. Our suffering can be reduced when we remember that we all experience suffering, so we're all in this human condition together. *We're not alone in our pain and suffering.* When we're comparing ourselves to others or are looking at someone else as not having any problems, it's important to remember that everyone has problems, and feels pain, suffering, and unhappiness. *Everyone!*

There's a beautiful, famous, American singer named Alicia Keys. She has a beautiful song about the suffering in life called *The Life*. It's very insightful and shows her wisdom. The song talks about the struggles of everyday life, her not understanding why she's trying so hard, the problems with finding a partner she can trust, and how she is just doing what she needs to do for survival (Keys, 2001). It seems to me that she is saying in the song that she doesn't want to continue a life that's nothing more than suffering.

> **LET'S STOP FOR A MINUTE. Let's think about this.** *Alicia Keys suffers? How is it that a person who has so much could suffer?* **Stop now and think. WHIGO?** *Think about Alicia Keys' song.* **But** *what about you? Do you think someone like her can really experience suffering like you?*

It's interesting that a famous, successful, and beautiful person like Alicia Keys would be singing about suffering, but she does. This is because we all experience suffering; how else could she understand? In response to her thoughts about not wanting to continue a life that's nothing but suffering, I would like to say that yes, we all have struggles and know suffering, *but* there is a way to reduce our suffering and find *more to live for.* A lasting, stable happiness *is* possible.

Because we're all human, we all have known some type of suffering, whether it's mental, emotional, physical, or spiritual, if for no other reason than things change. I have a friend who has said to me often that she hates change. We have talked about the fact that change is something in life that can't be prevented. The body changes, people around us change, the weather changes, and on and on. Nothing stays just the same. In fact, according to science, if something stops changing it no longer exists. Change causes stress in people, so it causes some level of suffering.

2) There's a sadness that we all experience as part of our human experience.

I remember when I was working as a psychotherapist, had just gotten a divorce (so I could no longer blame my husband for my unhappiness), and had started going through the grief that goes with the ending of a relationship. I was happy to be out of the relationship, but there was a sadness that I felt. As I went through my own therapy I saw that this sadness didn't change.

One evening I left a visit with a very good friend and went home. Sitting alone at home I started to cry. I was thinking that no one really cared about me and that I was totally alone. I then felt a heavy loneliness (feeling this loneliness even though I still had my father, several long-term, very good friends, and my siblings). At that time, I was still buying into the mistaken belief that I needed a man to be happy (although somewhere deep inside I knew I was happier without the responsibility of worrying about what another person needed, wanted, etc.). As I sat with this feeling, I started to reach into that deep part that's in all of us, that's always alone. After all, the only way for someone to really understand us and give us what we need is to be us. *We are the only one in our body, so we'll always be alone to some degree.* Over time, I became aware that this feeling of loneliness came from telling myself that it wasn't okay to be alone. As my awareness increased, I stopped being afraid of these thoughts and feelings and embraced them. They then started to go away. There's a saying, "What you resist, persists." As I let myself experience these thoughts about being alone and the loneliness they created, I was no longer afraid. I can still feel this loneliness at times, but I know it, I'm comfortable with it, and I know the pitfalls and the mistaken beliefs that produce this feeling. Because of becoming aware of, experiencing and becoming comfortable with my loneliness, it is no longer heavy. The loneliness that comes from thinking that I'm alone, rarely comes up for me now.

> **LET'S STOP FOR A MINUTE. Let's think about this.** *I was aware of feeling sad and lonely. Was my sadness coming from thinking I was alone or feeling lonely?* **Stop now and think. WHIGO?** *I had these feelings.* **But** *what about you? Are you aware of feeling any sadness or loneliness? Is it possible to have many people in your life and still think you are alone and feel lonely? Is it possible to be alone and not lonely?*

As my fears about being alone and my feeling of loneliness decreased, I noticed that my sadness remained. I then started to watch others to see if they seemed sad or depressed. I saw that even those who seemed on the surface to be happy showed a sadness in the moments that they weren't joking, weren't talking, or weren't distracted from themselves in some way. I started to ask my psychology co-workers if they experienced this depression. "Do you think there is a depression that we all have that just goes with being a human being?" Most told me that they hadn't thought about it. At this point of my exploration I wasn't using the term sadness. I was using the term depression.

As I continued to explore whether or not others saw this depression in themselves, or in others, I didn't find anyone who did. Farther along in this exploration, I was talking about this depression with a psychiatrist who I worked with. He said that he didn't think that it was depression, but rather a sense of sadness. I was overjoyed to learn that he had seen this sadness in others also. I then began to look more for the presence of sadness. Depression is a much heavier sadness. Just by going through the motions of work, relationships, change, illness, and anything else that can cause us stress, there is a sadness that we all experience just by having to deal with life. There's a sadness that goes with the suffering that's part of our human experience, a sadness that comes from being alone in our bodies with our experiences. I know that many people who experience this sadness don't realize they aren't alone, and that the sadness is normal. Because some people are unaware that it's normal to feel this way, they end up on antidepressant medication unnecessarily. A pill, though, can't relieve us of our experience of being human. Our belief that we are alone in this sadness can cause us to try to get rid of it in outside ways. Maybe we use drugs, sex, music, the internet, our phone, or reading; the choices to try to escape this sadness are endless. How can we escape something that is a normal part of our human experience?

If we understand that this sadness is a part of our common human experiences, this understanding can help to reduce our suffering, and make it less heavy. I've totally accepted this sadness, so I can testify that it can be greatly reduced. This sadness can be reduced to seeming more like a normal bump in the road, not a heavy sadness or depression. I still feel the suffering that goes with change and so forth, but it's less like sadness and more like a bump in the road that goes with life. A stronger feeling of sadness comes up more for me now when I am unhappy with the behavior of someone else. This is a different issue for me to look at and work on; it's an issue from another of my mistaken software programs.

3) We all want someone to understand how we truly, completely feel.

My clients have often said that they just want someone to understand. They just want someone in their life who cares enough to truly understand how they feel and to completely understand them. Often when working with couples this is an issue that comes up. "If you really care about me, you'll be able to completely understand how I feel, if you just try."

LET'S STOP FOR A MINUTE. Let's think about this. *Is it possible for someone to truly understand how we feel or think about something? Can someone completely understand us?* **Stop now and think. WHIGO?** *Most of us want someone to truly, completely understand us,* **but** *do you think this is possible? Have you ever been unhappy with someone because they couldn't or didn't seem to try to really understand you?*

We can understand pain, suffering, happiness, and most of the emotions that people feel, because we're human beings and have experienced most of them. Without someone's experiences, though, their inner programs, we can't totally, completely, or truly understand how they feel. *The only way we can totally, truly, and completely understand how someone feels, is to be them.* This doesn't mean that we can't feel for them or that we haven't had similar feelings or experiences; but again our experiences are from our view, our inner programs. We can never see through another person's eyes completely, totally, so we can never truly feel or understand what they feel. This is a secret discussed here because it's common for us to want others to *totally, truly, and completely* understand how we feel; *but* this is impossible. If we hold on to this unrealistic, unachievable desire we'll only increase our suffering. It's an outside search for a support and an understanding that's impossible for anyone to achieve.

4) We all get confused about the world around us.

Remember when I told you about telling my co-workers I was going to write a book called "What the hell is going on?" because that was the question I heard asked all day long? Well, it isn't just people in therapy who are asking this question. We all do. We've all heard someone talk about being confused about something that happened. We've all experienced this confusion ourselves. How many times have we wondered why something was happening, why did this person do what they did, why don't they love me, or just "What the hell is going on?" These are just some of the questions that we ask about our world.

> **LET'S STOP FOR A MINUTE. Let's think about this.** *All people get confused about the world. What about world leaders, famous people, and religious leaders?* **Stop now and think. WHIGO?** *Is it possible that all people get confused about the world?* **But** *what about you? Have you ever been confused about why someone did or said something? Have you ever been confused about situations that happen in the world?*

Sometimes our questions can be more complicated, such as the issue of our belief in God. I can't tell anyone the truths about the universe. If I tried, it would just be my opinion and not fact. When it comes to explaining our human condition, though, I can safely say that my observations are factual and would be difficult for anyone to dispute. The only way to never experience confusion about our world, especially when dealing with other people, would be to always know what everyone we meet is thinking and feeling. Further, to avoid being confused about the behavior of people in the world, we would need to know the thoughts and feelings of every living being. When we take our discussions beyond the area of people, it then becomes impossible to answer the questions. After all, who can answer the question for sure as to the particular time or place that an earthquake is going to happen? When we come to know the secrets in this book and start to observe them in our world, this knowledge, along with the answers in section three, will help decrease our confusion.

In PART ONE: Lasting, Stable Happiness, we talked about how most of our confusion is the result of believing in two false beliefs. These beliefs are that we're alone in our human condition and that a lasting, stable happiness can be found outside of ourselves through others and through possessions. Until we understand that these two beliefs are false we will remain confused. When we begin to understand that we aren't alone in our human experiences and that a lasting, stable happiness can only be found through an inner path, then our unhappiness and confusion will decrease. Our suffering decreases and our happiness increases.

5) We all feel insecure at times.

Someone who we might think would never feel insecure would be former American president Bill Clinton. President Clinton let people know that while he was growing up, his stepfather was an alcoholic, and that he would, at times, rescue his mother from bad situations. From a therapy point of view, someone in an alcoholic family becomes someone who helps the family patterns to continue, tries to make everyone okay, or has alcohol or drug problems themselves, or a combination of these characteristics.

President Clinton put out a tremendous amount of

effort to be successful in his life, and he was. In America, most people would say that becoming president is the greatest success. Do you remember when he first took office? He initially upset a lot of the old-timers on Capitol Hill because he didn't do what they wanted. He chose to do things his way. Well, it didn't take long before he started to have problems for trying to do things his way. At one point the news media and certain members of the House and Senate were making statements about how he couldn't make a decision about anything: in his situation he was damned whichever way he turned. If we can understand that in his family, President Clinton was possibly the one who tried to make everyone okay, along with being an idealist wanting to improve the world, then we can start to see why he couldn't make a decision. In his family he might have taken on the role of a pleaser or caretaker, the one who just tried to make everything all right for everyone. If we can't please or make everyone okay whichever way we turn, how do we decide what to do? Of course, after a few days he bit the bullet and went for it. But for a short time it is possible that he was hesitant because of his learned family patterns. How could he make a decision if some of the people he wanted to please and to think highly of him might be unhappy with his decisions? Of course, what I am presenting is my take on this situation. Having seen this behavior so many times in people with alcoholic family patterns, I thought I could instantly answer his critics' question, "Why can't he make a decision about anything?" If my analysis is correct, then President Clinton was feeling insecure, so he was having trouble deciding what to do.

One might say, "Well I know so and so and I'm sure they never feel insecure." In Secret Behaviors number one (We all wear a mask to the world at times) we'll talk about masks people wear; masks refer to the face we show to the world to hide what's really going on inside of us. The facial expressions and behavior choices that someone shows on the outside are the only clues that we have about what they may or may not be thinking or feeling. How many times have we been insecure and tried to hide it in some way?

> **LET'S STOP FOR A MINUTE. Let's think about this.** *Is it possible that someone who was able to become president of the United States could ever be insecure? What about the people we've met who we think are never insecure?* **Stop now and think. WHIGO?** *Think about others' insecurities.* **But** *what about you? Have you ever met someone who seemed totally secure, only for them to tell you something later that showed just how insecure they are? Have you ever felt insecure? Do you show your insecurities to others?*

For women, who is a better example of our human insecurities than Great Britain's Princess Diana? She was every little girl's fantasy: the beautiful woman who married her prince; a rich, beautiful, famous, compassionate princess. I think one of the reasons she was called "the people's princess" was that she showed us her insecurities, her humanness. She showed us her struggle with weight. She showed us her insecurities about her looks. She showed us the insecurities she had with her husband. If she was anorexic or bulimic, as was reported about her, then this would be a sign of her feeling like there was nothing she could control. Now if a rich, beautiful, famous woman from a "noble" family can be insecure, how is it possible that we simple, average women aren't?

Anyone who's honest will tell us that they feel insecure at times. I don't care how successful they have been in their lives. Remember the Alicia Keys' song, *The Life*, where she sings about her unhappiness and insecurities? In Secret Thoughts number one (We all think that there is something wrong with us, that we are incomplete) we'll also talk about the insecurities of the famous singer Whitney Houston.

We may not feel insecure at work or at home or in different situations in which we're comfortable, but there are situations in which we all feel uncomfortable, insecure. Maybe we're uncomfortable or insecure meeting new people, starting a new job, having dinner with the boss, trying to work out a business deal, or going out on a first date. Hopefully, we can understand people's insecurities better when we read the secrets about people's masks (Secret Behaviors one through three). A mask is used to protect ourselves. If we aren't feeling insecure, there's no need for protection. If we're trying to protect ourselves, it's usually about protecting how we feel about ourselves, our self-esteem. This behavior is an effort to protect the deeper mask, the mask we wear with ourselves, even if we're not aware of it.

In Secret Thoughts one and five (We all feel there is something wrong with us, that we are incomplete, and We are taught we are incomplete and need outside things for happiness and completion) we'll talk about how thinking we're incomplete causes us to feel insecure. We'll also talk about how the more secure we feel about ourselves, the higher our self-esteem is, and the less these concerns and worries come up. If we're feeling uncomfortable in some way with someone or in some situation, then we're feeling insecure and our self-esteem is being threatened in some way.

I keep using the examples of famous people because these are people we want to be, aspire to be like, or just envy. It's important to see that they suffer from this human condition just like we do. We could take any famous artist and just discuss the idea of "stage fright." Most, if they're honest, will tell us that even if it's only with their work, they worry about what others think. They'll tell us they're insecure about whether their work will be successful. How can they not worry about whether people will like what they do? After all, if people don't like their work, then they don't buy it. If their work doesn't sell, then it's possible their success and fame will be gone. We've all heard stories about famous performers having stage fright. If they weren't worried about what others thought, they would have nothing to fear. After the actress Meryl Streep won an Oscar in 2012, I heard her say on the television show *Entertainment Tonight* that all actors feel insecure.

6) We all want to be happy.

After I graduated from nursing school, one of my teachers came to work on the hospital unit where I worked. One day she said that what she really wanted was to get a higher degree. She then asked me what I really wanted. I remember very clearly saying, "I just want to be happy." This is *the bottom line*. Almost every action we take is about wanting to be happy. Take the person who robs a store. His goal is to get money. Why does he need money? He needs money to get things that will help him in some way. Often it's not just about food or shelter but is about being able to buy something he thinks will make his life better, something that will make him happy.

> **LET'S STOP FOR A MINUTE. Let's think about this.** *Why do we make the choices we do? Is there another reason other than wanting happiness? Can all choices be connected back, somehow, to wanting to be happy?* **Stop now and think. WHIGO?** *Think about why people make certain choices.* **But** *what about you? What is really the reason behind most of your choices? What is the bottom line? Why do you choose the things you do?*

Have you ever met someone who's unhappy all the time and seems to want to make everyone else unhappy? Well, of course, we all have. There are many reasons that this person may be acting this way. It could be depression or feeling hurt. Maybe it's the confused, mistaken belief that many people have, that we can feel better about ourselves by hurting others in some way. Many of us have the mistaken belief that by making ourselves look superior to someone, by hurting someone's feelings, or by just making fun of someone, we can feel better about ourselves. Sometimes we aren't even aware that we're doing this, because it's coming from an automatic pattern or software program. Usually this type of program is about protecting our self-esteem somehow. It may work for a short time; but if we have a conscience, we only end up feeling worse about ourselves by harming others. The bottom line is that we all want to be happy; we just get confused about how to make it happen.

Maybe taking drugs will make us happy. The only problem with this method is that if drugs make us happy then the only way to keep this happiness is to stay high all the time. As our body becomes more familiar with a drug, we have to take more and more to get the same effect. After a while the drug rules us, we don't rule the drug. We're addicted. Maybe it's food that will make us happy. Well, if this is so, then we have to eat all the time to stay happy. This attempt at happiness just creates an addiction to food. We all know the negative effects on our health by being overweight. No matter what thing or person we look to for our happiness, the only way to keep this happiness all the time is to have that thing or person with us all the time. This is one of my reasons for writing this book: to help people understand that a lasting happiness can't be found with outside things. We all know that it's impossible to have something or someone with us all the time. If we look for happiness in this way, we're bound to be unhappy when we don't have our object of happiness.

So you might say that we have to have many things and people that make us happy. Well, collecting many objects and people can be helpful; but what happens when a person dies or the thing wears out, or we've made ourselves sick from overuse of food, drugs, or other things? Can we now see how we're all on a constant search for happiness? It's like an animal's constant search for food. We're looking for some outside food to make us happy. In the answers section we'll talk about how to find a happiness that doesn't depend on things outside of us, that doesn't go up and down so much (it becomes more stable), and that lasts. In Secret Thought number five (We're taught we're incomplete and need outside things for happiness or completion) we'll talk more about how our happiness can change quickly when we depend on other people and objects to make us happy. In the following secrets we'll talk about how nothing outside of us has the power to make us happy. Something can make us happy only if we decide that it does. Others can't control us or make us think, feel, or do anything, so they aren't responsible for how we feel, whether it's happy or unhappy.

7) We all can feel complete. We just have to do the work to make it happen.

If we believe what has already been talked about, then we can begin to understand certain ideas. We can understand that if we're willing to look at ourselves, to come to know ourselves, and to allow ourselves to feel the feelings we have kept bottled up, then over time we can feel complete. After all, we're already complete. We just have to clear away the clutter or software programs that are getting in the way of us knowing and experiencing it. I'll discuss how we come to think and believe, and thereby feel incomplete in Secret Thoughts one and five (We all think that there is something wrong with us, that we are incomplete, and We are taught that we are incomplete and need outside things for happiness or completion).

This work isn't easy of course. In fact, sometimes we might feel worse before we feel better; but this is only temporary. Our reward is increased happiness, limited only by ourselves, and an inner freedom and spaciousness that we've never felt before. To me it has been well worth the trouble. Of course, I haven't reached the level of always feeling complete. I'm on the road, though. Having been on this road for some time, I have been blessed with having others in my life that are also on this journey. We talk often about the journey, and how happy we are that we took it. I'll share in more detail in the answers section some specific ways to help us on this journey.

8) We all want someone to care about us, to be loved.

One summer when I had returned to the USA from Asia, I was working on a psychiatric hospital unit. One day I was assigned to a female patient who we had to watch closely because she was having a lot of problems. At one point I didn't see her, so I went out on the porch to look for her. She was sitting on the cold floor. I helped her up, and she sat down in a chair. I sat next to her on the arm of the chair, and she laid her head on my leg. My heart went out to her because she was suffering so much. I then began to pat her on the back. I didn't work regularly on this unit, so it was several weeks before I saw her again. When I saw her again, she seemed to be doing better. As time went on, she became better and better. I noticed that her medication hadn't been changed, so I wondered what had happened for her to improve so much. One day I asked her. She looked at me, smiled, and said, "Remember the day you sat on the arm of my chair and patted me on my back?" I told her I did. She then said, "All I needed was some kindness and you showed me kindness. Thank you."

This woman continued to progress quickly and was able to be more and more independent. This is a story that shows the power of kindness. We all want someone to care about us.

> **LET'S STOP FOR A MINUTE. Let's think about this.** *How is it that a simple act of kindness could be so powerful that it helped this woman so much?* **Stop now and think. WHIGO?** *This woman said her progress was because of an act of kindness.* **But** *what do you think? Have you ever felt helped by someone's kindness? Is kindness the same as love?*

If someone tells us that they don't want anyone to love or care about them, then they're probably not telling the truth. It may be true that we don't want to pay a certain price to get someone's love, but that's different than not wanting someone to care about or love us. When a baby's born, if they don't get some kind of caring or nurturing from someone, they develop a condition called "failure to thrive." In a hospital, the staff would observe that the baby becomes increasingly unresponsive and at some point, if something isn't done, the baby will die. I'm not talking about dying from lack of food or water. I am talking about dying from the lack of loving contact with another person. There are research studies in which a baby monkey has been placed with a fake mother. Another baby monkey is placed with a real mother. The difference between how they thrive is great. The response of the baby with the real mother is much more positive. When we're older, we won't die from lack of this type of contact. Studies have shown, though, that positive physical, mental, or emotional contact with others does help to improve our mental, emotional, and physical health. Of course this is another attempt to get our needs met outside of ourselves, but we aren't talking about happiness here. We're talking about believing that someone thinks we're worth caring about. Believing that someone thinks we are worth caring about has a big effect on our self-esteem until we develop a strong, independent sense of self, and thereby gain high self-esteem.

Here's the time to talk about the tendency that we have to try to get people who don't seem to like or care about us, to like and care about us. When I was in my early twenties I began hanging out with a popular but negative group of people from work. There was another group of people there who seemed to like me very much. This other group seemed to be made up of very kind and caring people, but they weren't part of the popular group. This other group made a lot of effort to be my friend. I didn't return their attention much. I continued to put more energy into being with the popular group. At one point I saw that I wasn't happy with this popular group, so why was I making an effort to be with them? I looked very closely at my behavior and thinking, and made a decision. I decided to spend time with the caring people because I didn't have to put out a lot of energy to be loved and accepted. I reduced the time I spent with the "popular" people and found myself to be much happier. Both groups accepted me, but one was supportive and the other wasn't.

LET'S STOP FOR A MINUTE. Let's think about this.
Can you *see how I was with a group that wasn't support-*

ive only because they were considered "the popular" group? **Stop now and think. WHIGO?** *Think about what was going on inside of me that I chose a group that wasn't supportive.* ***But*** *what about you? Have you ever tried to be with the "popular" group even though you could see that they weren't positive people? Have you ever chosen to be with someone because they were the more "hip" or "popular" person instead of being with someone who wasn't hip or popular but was really supportive and seemed to care for you?*

It's important to find those who will support us. Think of the times we've found ourselves putting out extra energy to belong to a certain group, or to get someone to be our friend, or to get someone to love us. Many of us have seen couples where one person in the relationship seems to be the kind and caring one and the other seems unkind and often manipulative. From a therapist view, this is about the person who seems kind and caring trying to get the other one to love them. This thinking is often about "If I can just get them to love or care about me then that means I'm loveable and worth caring about; if I can't get them to love or care about me then I'm not loveable." This thinking comes from the "kind" person's inner programs or patterns, their software programs, most likely their programs about their self-esteem. Something in their programs causes them to try to get someone, whose programs are so different from their own, to love them. The answer to the question of why someone behaves in a certain way with someone else has to do with that person's learned inner programs, their software programs. It has little to nothing to do with the other person. Bottom line, each of us is coming from the learned thought-feeling patterns on our inner programs.

It's important to look at this idea that we can only feel better about ourselves by getting a particular person or group to care about us. This thinking is about low self-esteem. What about the people who already love and care about us and do so easily? After all, are we not worthy of this? Does it mean there's something wrong with those who accept and love us easily? Is it true that only certain people can make us feel better about ourselves? Well, in Secret Behaviors number seven (No one can make us think, feel, say, or do anything) we'll talk about the truth that no one can make us think, feel, or do anything. *I guarantee that we're all loveable.* We need to not fall into the negative pattern of believing that we can only prove that we're loveable by getting someone who doesn't seem to care about us, to care about us. *There's not something wrong with us if they don't care about us. We don't control the inner programs in their minds; therefore, we can't control their view of us. We aren't what they see. They only see what we show them. Even then, they see us in their own specific way, from their own specific, inner programs. We can't be all things to all people.*

The most exhausting thing I have seen people attempt is trying to be all things to all people because they want everyone to like them. The only way to get everyone to like us is to be all things at all times. There's a nurse that I worked with who always said to people what she thought they wanted to hear. The problem was that different people felt differently about some things. When she was with two people with different views, it was interesting to watch her say nothing. She would be quiet; otherwise she might upset someone. Say there's the person who enjoys quiet people, then there's the person who likes to party. How are we going to get both of these people to like us? We would have to be opposites at times. How can we pull that off if we're with them at the same time? We can try, but think of how exhausting it would be to change how we behave to such a degree. It works better to decide what we like or value and then find people to be with who like or value the same things. When we do this we will find that many people find us easy to love.

III

Secret Thoughts

1) We all think there's something wrong with us, that we're incomplete.

Once I was in northern California attending a self-development course. Out of the sixty people in there, I was the least educated and made less money than most of them; this was after I had my master's degree and had been working as a psychotherapist. As everyone began to share, it became clear that every person believed that there was something wrong with them. They all shared ways in which they thought that something was missing, that they were incomplete somehow, or that something was wrong with them. From the outside these people all seemed to be "successful": doctors, lawyers, museum curators, and so forth. They were all highly educated and most had six-figure incomes. I had already had "successful" individuals come to me and share the belief that they were incomplete, that something was missing, or that something was wrong with them. I always found it surprising that they also thought they were the only ones who felt this way. Even I was surprised, though, to learn that each individual at this course, including myself, felt this way. After all, these were not just "successful" people, but people searching and trying to improve themselves. Here I was, though, hearing first-hand how they were feeling. I couldn't deny this truth.

Sometimes we look around at others and think, "I wish I was them." This thinking goes with the saying, "The grass is always greener on the other side." We look at others and think they have it all, they have it all together, or maybe they're really happy. We then wish to be this other person or to have what we think this other person has outwardly or inwardly. We wish to be this other person in an effort to be rid of this feeling of being incomplete or having something wrong with us.

> **LET'S STOP FOR A MINUTE. Let's think about this.** *Does a person who seems to have it all, feel complete and totally secure within themselves?* **Stop now and think. WHIGO?** *You can think about how others might be feeling,* **but** *what about you? Have you ever felt like something was missing inside of you? Have you ever felt like something is wrong with you? Have you ever wished you were someone else?*

This next story I heard second hand, so I can't say that it's true; but it didn't surprise me. I was told that Nobel Peace Prize winner, His Holiness the Dalai Lama, was once meeting with a group of famous scientists, a favorite thing for him to do I've heard. After they talked about science, they began a more general conversation. He was asked by one scientist about this feeling of being incomplete, insecure, or like something was missing. I was told that His Holiness replied, "Surely you don't feel insecure, with all your accomplishments?" Reportedly, every scientist there said they had this feeling of insecurity. I believe this story because this feeling of being incomplete, that something is missing or that something is wrong with us, is about our level of self-esteem. It doesn't matter how much we have outwardly accomplished. If someone hasn't done the inner work needed to get high self-esteem, it doesn't matter what they have accomplished, they can still have low self-esteem.

Let's look at the life of the famous singer and actress Whitney Houston. Whitney Houston died in February 2012. Although her funeral was closed to the public, many different news stations carried stories about what happened at the funeral. One story shown repeatedly was the actor Kevin Costner talking about his experiences with Whitney when they were filming the movie *The Bodyguard*. He said, "She had doubt ... Am I good enough? Am I pretty enough? Will they like me?" (Dray 2012). How could such a beautiful and successful artist have such self-doubt? It's because until we do the work to understand where these feelings come from, we will continue to wonder if something is wrong with us or whether we are incomplete, and our self-esteem will continue to be low. This directly addresses another secret. The one about how we are programmed. Until we do the work of looking inside, even we don't know a lot about our inside programs. Our self-esteem is the view we have of ourselves, which comes from our inner programs.

2) We're programmed at a young age to believe what others say about us is true.

Remember the television commercial I shared with you in the lasting, stable happiness section? This commercial speaks directly about, as the caption said, "Your children are what you tell them they are." We have talked before about the idea that our experiences are like software programs put on our inner hard drive. This software is made up of the programs that we use to see ourselves and the world. When we are born, we totally depend upon whoever is caring for us. Without someone else to help us, we would die from starvation, lack of warmth, lack of water, or failure to thrive. When we start to grow, people tell us different things about ourselves. They may say things like, "Oh, she's so pretty. He's so handsome. He/she is such a good/bad child," and on and on. As we continue to grow and develop more skills, we're taught how to walk, how to talk, and many different things. Along with these skills, the people around us are constantly telling us who we are, good/bad, smart, pretty, ugly, stubborn, and on and on. These people are giving us food, shelter, comfort, and all the things that we seem to need to survive. We depend on them. Our dependence on these people makes them very powerful. If we tell them "no" they can simply pick us up and take us to our room or yell at us. It can be very frightening, and thereby powerful, when someone is so small and the large person is doing the yelling.

    My younger sister told me a story about my nephew. One Sunday they were in the middle of church services when my nephew, then three years old, said he had to have a bowel movement. My sister was irritated because this seemed to happen often and made her miss church, but she took her son to the bathroom. As she waited, she heard him praying to God, "Please help me go to the bathroom, so my mommy won't be mad at me." Cute story, yes, but I use it here to help us see how sensitive a small child is to their parents' behavior, reactions, words, or feelings: all of their expressions. We don't have to tell our child we think he's bad. All we have to do is yell at him or give him an angry look. All these experiences contribute to creating who we're going to become, which creates how we feel about ourselves, our self-esteem, and the world around us. My father never yelled, but easily controlled me with a look of disappointment or disapproval. I can remember thinking, "Just hit me or something. Just don't look at me that way."

> **LET'S STOP FOR A MINUTE. Let's think about this.** *Are our parents so powerful when we are growing up that we believe everything they tell us about ourselves?* **Stop now and think. WHIGO?** *Think about how my father and sister controlled their children,* **but** *what about yours? Can you remember a time when your parents told you who or what you were? Do you remember a time when your parents controlled you without saying anything to you? How did your parents control you? What about the positive and negative things they said about you?*

Keeping in mind what we just talked about, I want to ask a question: "Do you think that anyone can know what is inside of us without asking us?" The powerful, factual truth is that they can't. How can someone know who we are without seeing inside of us? As a child we know very little about the world and certainly don't know that we don't understand many things. It's very natural that we would believe the big, powerful people around us who are taking care of us. If no one can know what is inside of us unless we tell them, though, then how can these powerful people know and tell us who we really are? They can't. It's just their opinion. Their reaction to us at any given time shows what's going on inside of them, not us. Because of what we've been told we are, we have taken these childhood messages inside and see them as who or what we really are, as true. No one teaches us to question them unless maybe we seek therapy. Often these messages are so deeply held inside of us that they are difficult to see and to get rid of. *No one knows what's inside of us but us. We are not what people said or say we are.* How can they know us without seeing inside of us? Starting to understand that we are not what people have said or say we are and then starting to look at the messages (software programs) we have been given is the key to creating a strong, independent, confident self-esteem.

Some professionals believe that the personality is developed by the age of two. Others believe it's determined by our genes, and we come into the world with our personality. I say that no one has the proof of when or how we develop our personality, but I can promise you that two things are true. These are that our personality is affected by the environment that we grow up in and that nothing is permanent. If we want to change, we can change. We will discuss this idea further when we talk about the mistaken belief of being able to find our true self (Secret Thought number eight).

3) Everyone's inner make-up (hard drive) is programmed differently.

In the introduction I shared with you how differently my older sister and I reacted to our mother's death. We were both created by the same parents. We grew up in the same house. We went to the same schools. So many things in our environment were similar, yet we reacted so differently to the loss of our mother. Even though we were in the same environments, it wasn't possible for us to have the exact same experiences or the exact same messages from the world around us.

> **LET'S STOP FOR A MINUTE. Let's think about this.** *Think about how and why we see things differently from others.* **Stop now and think. WHIGO?** *Think about how my sister and I reacted so differently to our mother's death,* **but** *what about you? Do you and your brothers and sisters think alike? If you don't have siblings, do you think like your parents? Do your parents think like their parents? Have you ever gotten upset with someone because they didn't see something like you did?*

Our inner make-up can be easier to understand if we look at our genes. Obviously the only people who have the same genetic make-up are identical twins, but even identical twins don't have the same fingerprints. Also there's no way that they have the exact same experiences, and thereby the exact same memories tucked away in their brains. This is an important secret because most people never stop to think about or understand how we are all different. How often do we get irritated with people for not seeing something the same way as we do? It's impossible for anyone to see something exactly as we do because they have different inside programs. They may agree with something that we think, believe, or feel, but there's no way they can see it exactly as we do. This is very important for us to understand, so that we can use the tools in the answers section. Each one of us is totally unique. There will never be another person exactly like us, there will never be another person with our specific programs. This alone makes us special.

Even in the same household each child is treated differently. Even the most aware parent can't treat each child exactly the same, if for no other reason than children act differently. Even if this was possible to do, each child would still have a different memory of the event because of what's already on their inside programs. So yes, as human beings we share basic human wants, desires, needs, and feelings, but even these are specific to each person. For example, some people value relationships over possessions, others value possessions over relationships. We have different inner views because of our different, specific programs. Part of the reason that my older sister and I reacted differently to our mother's death was about how much we had physically matured. Some would argue it was based on our genes. My sister was thirteen years old with more mature skills at expression. I was eleven years old and, according to theories about how children mature, was not as mature in my ability to express my feelings. How can we explain my instinct to step up and care for my two younger siblings, while my older sister acted more distant? This is probably because of our different inside software programs.

4) No one knows what's going on inside of us but us.

My first job in psychology was on an adult inpatient psychiatric unit. One day a psychologist asked me how I was getting along with a certain client. I said I thought that our conversations were helping him. This psychologist then told me that the client had just been in his office and was talking about hurting me. This situation took me totally by surprise. This experience really drove home for me that we never really know what's going on in someone's mind. This may seem an extreme example, but it shows how people can look at interactions very differently. This is because our understanding of our world or experiences is from our inside programs.

> **LET'S STOP FOR A MINUTE. Let's think about this.** *Can someone really know what we are thinking or feeling if we don't tell them? What if they have known us very well for a long time?* **Stop now and think. WHIGO?** *Think about this story I just told you;* ***but*** *what about you? Have you ever had a situation where you thought someone was thinking one way and later found out they thought something else? Have you ever thought you knew what someone close to you was thinking, but when you talked with them about it, they were thinking differently?*

You say, "Okay, but it seems like my mother or my spouse knows what I am thinking. It seems like they can read my mind sometimes." Well yes, it's possible for someone to learn about us and pay enough attention to our facial expressions, patterns of behavior, and so forth to become good at guessing what we're thinking or feeling, but how can they really know? If we aren't telling them, then it's just a guess. Parents are good about guessing what their kids are thinking and feeling. After all, they had a major influence in programming us. But these guesses aren't the same as knowing. *No one knows what we are thinking and feeling unless we tell them; therefore, no one knows what is going on inside of us but us.*

Because of the way I do my spiritual practice, I'm often going through a store saying prayers. Do you think anyone knows that I'm praying while I'm shopping? I think not. I've joked with others about how I protect people from my thoughts all the time. By this I mean that when something happens with someone and negative thoughts come up in me, I keep them to myself, protecting the person from my negative mind. Do you think they're aware of this? I promise they aren't. They may pick up that I'm more irritable or quiet, but they can't know why unless I tell them. We've all done the same thing at some point by "biting our tongue."

5) We're taught we're incomplete and need things outside of ourselves for happiness or to feel complete.

When I was working in India, my co-workers often said that education was the answer to fixing most of the problems of the people we were working with. We were working in an area where people were poor and education was hard to get. We didn't have a television, and newspapers and magazines with current events were hard to get, so news about the world was hard to get. Sometimes we were invited to the home of a university professor who had a television. Once we watched the BBC news on the conflict in the Balkans, which showed pictures of refugees in Bosnia fleeing to safety. Because I hadn't seen anything on television about this war before, my ideas about what was going on there were from what little I could find to read about it. I had visions in my mind of refugees, like the refugees in Africa, walking hundreds of miles to safety with their families and only the possessions they could carry. When I saw the refugees fleeing Bosnian towns, some had cars with snow skis on top. They had warm clothing and many other physical comforts. Of course, I'm not saying this was the case for everyone. I'm only talking about what I saw on the BBC. I thought to myself that if it's true that education is the way to decrease people's problems and conflicts, how is it that these Western, more wealthy, and more educated people could be killing each other so easily?

To me, obviously education isn't the answer to everything, although I have heard people say this many times. Were the Nazis during World War II uneducated? No, many of them were very educated people. This is an example of something considered true that doesn't match up with what we see in the world. Will an education make you happy and complete? I can testify that it doesn't; at least not the type of academic education that people are saying will help. Yes, an academic education might help to increase the amount of money someone can make, and thereby their physical comfort, but what about our problems which don't involve money? Yes, this type of education can hopefully expand our thinking; but as we've talked about before, an intellectual understanding of something doesn't mean our understanding is increased. The type of education I'm talking about here, though, can be very helpful with decreasing conflicts and increasing our happiness. This is mainly because it's an education that has an inner, not outer, focus.

> **LET'S STOP FOR A MINUTE. Let's think about this.**
> *So education might not make us feel complete or happy, but what about all the other things? Can finding the right person, the right job, or the right place to live help us be happy and to feel that we are complete?* **Stop now and think. WHIGO?** *Think about whether things outside of us can give us happiness, make us feel complete, or create what we need to feel secure and happy;* **but** *what about you? Have you ever looked to another person or something else for happiness or to feel that you are secure and complete? Did this help you get the happiness you wanted or did it cause you suffering?*

We get messages from many different sources in our world. Advertisements and commercials on the television are big examples. Advertisers spend a lot of money to see what will get us to buy their products. Of course, many people in the field of advertising understand the secret that everyone feels insecure. What's a better way to influence us than to hook our insecurities, and then tell us their product will help us feel better? There was a jingle from an old television commercial that said Ultra Bright toothpaste would give our mouth sex appeal. Why do we need sex appeal? We need sex appeal to attract a partner, of course. After all, we all know that we can't be happy without a partner. Right? We need a partner for our life to be complete. Right? This is a strong message in most societies. It's in movies, songs, television programs, and advertising, and is often reinforced by the people in our lives. The answer to happiness is just finding the right partner, right? Wrong. Why do you think the divorce rate in America is so high? People get married, and after time we find out that we didn't marry a prince, a princess, or a perfect person: we married a human being. Instead of dealing with this directly, lots of us just think we made a mistake, that this was just not the right person. So we divorce and begin our search again.

Now let's consider physical objects. A lot of us believe that buying a car will increase our happiness. It does for a while, until we feel pressure to pay for it or someone scratches it. Remember the story I told you about the woman who was so happy to have a new car and then so unhappy after someone scratched it. The same can go for a house, clothes, vacations, and any physical object. They can only make us happy for a limited amount of time. We then have to go to our next physical object, or "fix," to get another rush of happiness. Limited happiness isn't what we are talking about in this book. We're talking about how to have lasting happiness: a lasting, stable happiness. *No person or thing can complete us. Nothing outside of us can give us lasting, stable happiness.* Looking to outside things for happiness means our happiness will depend on these things. If the outside thing changes in some way or goes away, then the happiness connected to it also changes or goes away. This is why I say this type of happiness is limited and not lasting. It will go away at some point. Nothing (people and objects) is permanent. Outside things won't exist at some point. They don't last. If we look to things for happiness, our happiness will also not last. It will go up and down, depending on our experience with the thing we are looking to for happiness and completion.

6) We all worry about what others think.

In my first psychotherapist job I was asked to run a series of personal growth groups with a co-worker. The groups were made up of educated, working, adult females. In one of these groups, a woman shared how she was worried about what someone thought about her at work. One of the other women responded, "You do that. I thought I was the only one who ever worried about what others thought." The other women joined in, and we discovered that they all worried about what others thought about them. My co-worker and I were very surprised to learn that these women each thought they were the only ones who felt this way.

> **LET'S STOP FOR A MINUTE. Let's think about this.**
> *Is it possible that everyone worries about what others think? What about those people who are so successful?* **Stop now and think. WHIGO?** *This story talks about just a few women;* **but** *what about you? Have you ever worried about what someone else thinks about you? Have you ever met someone who you think never worries about what others think?*

It is true that we don't worry as much about what a stranger thinks, as we do about the thoughts of our parents or someone important to us. Some people, though, even worry about what strangers think. If this isn't true, then why would we worry about what we look like when we're traveling? We could say it's about our self-esteem. This is true, but I say there's more. If we have high self-esteem we don't worry so much about what others think, in particular strangers. After all, if a stranger doesn't like how we look, what difference does it make? We'll probably never see them again.

I'm not saying that we all worry all the time about what everyone thinks. Most of us have different amounts of worry with different people. How much we worry about what someone thinks of us is about how we see that person or want them to see us. This worry is about our self-esteem. The more confident and trusting we are in ourselves, the less we worry about what others are thinking about us. This experience of worrying about what others think is another of those well-hidden things, a secret. It doesn't appear, though, to be as threatening to reveal to others as some of the other secrets.

I remember hearing the Tibetan teacher Gelek Rinpoche say once that if women aren't worried about what others think about them, then why do they wear makeup? I know women who won't leave the house without their makeup on because they're worried about what others will think about how they look. I know men who would never express their feelings for fear of being seen as weak. These are examples of worrying about what others think because of low self-esteem. If we weren't worried about what others thought, we wouldn't wear masks. We would be comfortable with showing our true self, at least to the level of our awareness, at all times.

OUR SECRETS Secret Thoughts

7) We believe if someone cares about us they'll know how we feel and think without us telling them.

There was a teenage client I worked with whose mother would come into her session at times. This girl grew up thinking that her mother sent her and her brother out with their father on the weekends because she wanted time away from them. In one session, her mother talked about sending the kids with their father on the weekends because he was always so busy, and she wanted them to spend more time with him. The girl was very surprised to hear what her mother said. This goes back to the mind reading we discussed previously. The only way that someone could know how we think or feel without asking us would be if they could read our minds. I don't know anyone who can really read someone's mind.

> **LET'S STOP FOR A MINUTE. Let's think about this.**
> *This girl had decided she knew why her mother sent her and her brother with their father on the weekends, but she was wrong. How many other situations do you think she has been wrong about?* **Stop now and think.** **WHIGO?** *Think about how this girl assumed she knew something without asking;* **but** *what about you? Have you ever thought you knew why someone did something only to find out you were wrong? Did this attempt at mind reading help you or cause you suffering?*

Probably the biggest mistaken belief that marriage and family therapists encounter is the belief that we don't have to tell a person we're in a relationship with what we're thinking or feeling. After all, "if they care about us they'll know." As a therapist, I've often been in sessions with people and helped them tell each other what they were thinking and feeling. Often people are surprised to find out that they've misunderstood something. I've often heard people say they knew what someone was thinking or feeling, and they'd never talked with this person about it. Come on, how can we really know what someone is thinking or feeling if they haven't told us? People will often say that because someone had a particular expression on their face or they acted a certain way, they knew what that person was thinking. Because of my family patterns, when I'm feeling sad my facial expression is often one of irritation. Yes, I may be feeling a little irritation, but that's not how I'm really feeling. Do you think anyone would read my expression as sadness? Just like when I'm shopping and saying prayers, no one really knows what's going on inside of me. If someone cares about us, it's true that they will spend time with us and try to get to know us. *They can't know what we are thinking or feeling, though, unless we tell them.* Anything else is just a guess. Think of the times when we've guessed wrong. Think about how unfair it is to expect someone to know something that it's impossible for them to know. Think of all the people who thought their marriage was in good shape only, to their surprise, to find out that their partner wanted a divorce. Many people were surprised when my ex-husband and I decided to get a divorce. Most people said they thought we were the perfect couple. That was because we didn't share or show our true feelings to anyone.

8) We believe it's possible to find or become our "true self."

Many times people have told me that they were going to some type of class to discover their true self. The idea is that they think if they "peel away the onion" enough they will find a one, unchanging, true self. There was a certain point on my journey that I strongly believed that I could discover my true self. I now believe this thinking to be a mistaken belief. I thought then, though, that if I could just work through certain issues, learn certain things about myself, and become in touch with my inner self that I would discover and become my "true self." By true self I'm not talking about our ability to become "enlightened or God-like" that some people believe is possible. I'm talking about the idea that we can discover our true personality, our true womanliness, or our true manliness: a solid known, unchanging, "true" self.

    Think about all the different emotions, attitudes, thoughts, and behaviors we experience in just one hour. Depending upon the situation, we can experience many different feelings and thoughts. I think the work environment is a good place to look at because we're involved with so many different people and situations. One moment we might feel happy and be patient and kind. The next, we may be unhappy and act in a negative or irritated way. We move between the two poles with the white on one end and the black on the other. We mainly operate in the gray between these two poles, but at times we may be on either extreme. We all have the ability to be kind (one extreme), and the ability to be cruel (the other extreme). It's about choices, and how we see and choose to react to the world around us. We're all these different things, the total of all these emotions and thoughts. We'll never be just one thing or one type of person, a one "true self," always this or that. To be this would require that we never change. Even basic science tells us that if the movement or changing within a living organism stops, that organism will no longer exist. So how could we possibly be one thing? We are changing and evolving at all times. The cells of our body die and grow continuously. We learn something or discover something new about ourselves and others all the time, which produces a change in who we are. Are we the same person we were twenty years ago, or ten years ago? Or even last month? Physically, it's obviously not true. It's interesting that we think that this can be true about "who we are" mentally, emotionally, or spiritually. I say it's not possible to find or become our one "true self." It's a mistaken belief. The truth is that we are an always-changing person: our cells are always changing and our mind is always experiencing things. To be a one, unchanging self would mean we would no longer exist.

IV

Secret Behaviors

1) We all wear a mask to the world at times.

A friend of mine was having some problems at work. One of her co-workers helped her move from the problem work area to work with her. My friend was very grateful for her kindness and saw this woman as a supportive friend whom she could trust. After some time, the co-worker started putting her work off onto my friend, was taking very long breaks, and became unkind. My friend talked about how much this woman's behavior had changed, and that she could no longer trust her. We talked about how it's not possible to know how this woman really was. Which was real, the kind woman or the unkind woman? Chances are this woman was wearing a mask at different times, and that the only way to really understand her would be for her to explain her behavior. Even then she might not be truthful.

LET'S STOP FOR A MINUTE. Let's think about this.
This woman presented herself differently to my friend at

different times. Can we really know how someone is just from how they present themselves? **Stop now and think. WHIGO?** *My friend thought she could trust this woman, then thought she couldn't;* **but** *what about you? Have you ever known someone to be one way and then seen them change? Have you ever had someone you thought was a friend then became someone who wasn't? Maybe it was the other way around; did your enemy become a friend?*

The mask I'm talking about in this secret is the behavior that we show to people and the world when we interact with them. How many of us show others how we truly are at all times? Those who've managed to shed their masks would agree that even they don't always show or say exactly what's on their minds. We aren't talking, though, about the mask of being pleasant or courteous to someone whom we don't like. There have been many times that I could have said what I thought, but I chose not to, and even sometimes lied, to avoid hurting someone's feelings. We're not talking here, though, about protecting others' feelings. That isn't what this secret is about. Here we're talking about the mask of self-protection, the mask that we wear to prevent being vulnerable to others and the world. The mask we wear to protect our self-esteem. How many times have we felt hurt by, insecure with, or in love with someone, and out of fear, didn't show our true feelings or thoughts? In other words, we have worn a mask to hide our insecurities and fear. This is the mask American teenagers are taking about when they call someone a poser or a pretender. A poser or pretender is someone who presents themselves to others in a certain way to try to get people to believe they are this way, even though they don't believe it themselves. They are posing, pretending, or showing us a certain mask.

Some people are very good at their masks. To most people they seem secure, very smart, or maybe like they "have it all together." If they haven't done the work to be secure from the inside, though, I promise you that the person is not secure. Let's talk about some of the types of masks that I have seen.

There is the mask I call the intellectual masturbator mask. This is the person who tells us about all the latest books they've read, all the trivia they know, or all the facts or pieces of information they can share about a subject to say, "Look how smart I am. Don't you think I'm great?" A man I worked with was talking about one of our co-workers. He said every time someone brought something up this person would join in to tell a similar story about himself. His story was usually about the experience that he had with the topic being discussed, and how much he knew about it. This behavior is about trying to get people to think that he knows a lot; but it's also a way of trying to get attention or to feel important, an attempt to increase his low self-esteem. This mask can be displayed several ways, not just through intellectual things. It could also be by showing people all the popular possessions we have like clothes or bags. "See, I have this name brand possession. Doesn't this mean something awesome about me?" It could be through talking about all the places we've traveled. "See how worldly I am. Doesn't this mean something great about me?" Whatever form this mask takes, it's all about trying to get someone to think good things about us. It's about our low self-esteem. It's about a need to protect ourselves from others learning that we feel insecure.

One of the most powerful masks I've seen, and the one that seems to make others feel the most insecure, is the superior critic mask. This mask can be shown as an obvious critic or a more hidden critic. The hidden critics, if they are skillful, don't have to directly criticize or put down someone. This mask is the most powerful when it's done in the hidden way. People seem to feel more insecure with the hidden critic than the obvious critic. For example, the hidden critic will make certain kinds of statements. "A lawyer friend of mine is such a good lawyer, but he just can't seem to find a date," or, "My friend married this guy she met when she was traveling in Europe, but now she's so unhappy." The mask here is to say, "Look at the great friends that I have. They are highly educated or world travelers yet look at the problems they have. Too bad they don't have it together like I do." Now this mask is very powerful because people then compare themselves with this type of masked person and see themselves as less. "Why don't I have such cool friends? How is it that they are so together?" It's a subtle way to build oneself up while making others feel less. I've seen this mask used many times and watched as others seem to shrink, wondering why their life is less.

There are as many types of masks as there are people; the intellectual masturbator and critic are just a couple of common masks. Just how often we wear a mask is really about how strong our self-esteem is; the lower the self-esteem, the greater the need for the mask for protection. When I decided to get a divorce, many people were surprised. They had no idea that my husband and I were having problems. Guess why? It was because we both wore the happiness mask. After all, we didn't want people to get a clue about the true suffering we were experiencing in our relationship. We both were protecting ourselves from the possible negative things people might say about us. I had someone say to me how they thought "you two had the perfect relationship." This story is an example of how we judge a person by their outer mask, and how little we really know about what is going on inside of them.

I'm not saying that it's always bad to wear a mask. Sometimes it's necessary for protection, but most of the time it isn't. Let me share a couple of stories about when a mask is really needed for protection. There's a young woman I know who was ten or eleven when the Communist government era ended in her country of Romania. Before that she said she was told, "Don't share your real feelings with anyone. It can be dangerous." It was dangerous because if the government didn't like what you said they might arrest you. How sad to think that the only place she could show or express her true self was when she was in her home. She wore a mask out of a true need for protection. The second story is from a book I read about three generations of women growing up in China, before and then during the communist government control. It's a true story written by a woman, who is my age, about her, her mother, and her grandmother. This woman wrote about never knowing when someone might accuse her or someone in her family of something, and they would go to prison. She wrote about how they couldn't speak openly about what they were thinking or feeling out of the fear of someone telling lies about what they had said. I cried as I thought about how at the times she had these worries, my main worry was whether I was going to have a date to what I thought was an important school dance. These people's masks were very important for their protection.

What I'm talking about here is understanding that most people are protecting themselves most of the time. We aren't protecting ourselves from being arrested, imprisoned, or physically harmed like in the stories of the women from Romania and China. We're protecting ourselves from people finding out that we're insecure and vulnerable. By understanding this, we can begin to watch and be less threatened ourselves by what we see. Is what a person showing us really who they are, or are they just showing us their mask? By asking these questions we take the first step to no longer comparing ourselves to others. Comparing ourselves to others leads us to feel less than or insecure with them. We can also become familiar with the mask that we show to the world. As we come to know our mask better, we can also become more aware of the tremendous amount of energy it takes to continue with it. I was talking with a co-worker about how I thought it must take a lot of energy for someone to hide themselves from others and to pretend to be something different than they are. To my surprise she replied, "It does."

Once I asked a woman I worked with about some negative statements I had been told she said about me. She said that she could usually figure out what people want or need and then she would help them with it. She then said that she couldn't figure me out. I told her this was because what you see is what you get. Because I didn't wear a mask, there was nothing to figure out. I think this was hard for her to understand because this wasn't what she normally saw. She was much more aware of the face or mask people wore. She based her relationships with people on being able to see past their masks and then get on their good side by supporting them where they were vulnerable. I also had a fellow therapist tell me the same thing once. She said she could usually figure out what people wanted or needed and then would set about helping them get it, but she couldn't figure me out. Both of these people were, on some level, aware of people's masks. The problem for them was that they believed that people's masks were real. They believed that people were what they showed to the world. I'm saying that most people are not as they show themselves.

Most of us are aware that although we appear to show ourselves in one way, inside we don't feel this way. I use the following example frequently when explaining masks to people. Let's say we go to a party. When we walk in, standing in the corner all alone is the most gorgeous woman we have ever seen. She isn't smiling and seems a little anxious and full of herself. What do you think is going on with her? Most people say, "Well she thinks she's better than everyone else. She's all about herself." I reply that if this woman was as confident and full of herself as they think, then she would be acting differently. Think of how we act when we're with people and feeling confident and when we're with people and feeling insecure. When a person is confident and comfortable with themselves they are the life of the party, not standing alone looking unhappy. Maybe you don't believe this. I can tell you, though, that from my clients, people I have known in personal growth situations, and people who have come to me in general, *people don't show us how they really feel most of the time. Almost everyone wears a mask.* People who are secure are usually friendly, kind, and empathetic. They don't try to get us to think certain things about them. The greater these qualities are, the greater is the level of the person's self-esteem. This is not to ignore the mask of being the kind, loving, self-sacrificing person. This mask is often a deeper kind of mask, though, which we will discuss in the next secret.

2) We all wear a mask with ourselves at some level.

Once a client told me that she thought I was so strong and that she admired me because I was always taking care of others. I remember smiling and saying, "That's strong to you. That's easy for me. Strong for me is letting you take care of me." I said this because I knew that taking care of others was my way of being in control and getting my needs met. As a psychotherapist, I've always felt that part of my work was to understand my own issues, so I didn't put them on my clients. After all, my clients had enough to deal with without having to deal with my issues. By looking at myself, I discovered this deep pattern that I had learned in my family about how to get attention and love. It was a mask that took me a long time to discover. With this pattern, letting others take care of me would have meant feeling out of control and vulnerable. If I started to look to them to get my needs met, they might not be there for me some day. They might leave me. This is why I developed the unconscious pattern, mask, of taking care of others, so that they stayed in my life because they thought they needed me. Can you see my control issues?

> **LET'S STOP FOR A MINUTE. Let's think about this.** *Can you see how I developed the mask of being the strong person who took care of others, not to really care for them, but to meet my needs for attention and love? Can you see that what others thought was strength was really fear? Fear of others not being there for me.* **Stop now and think. WHIGO?** *Think about how I developed this deep mask of taking care of others out of fear and my needs for love and attention;* **but** *what about you? How did you learn to get your needs met when you were a child? Are you aware of any patterns you have that may really be about something other than what is obvious to you? Are these patterns helping you, or causing you some problem?*

The mask that we wear with ourselves is a more hidden mask, a mask that's on a deeper level. It can take a lot of inner self work to see it. See, we all have a view of ourselves that we show to the world. Part of this is our protective mask that we often know. The other part is the way we show ourselves to others, the way we want others to see us, and how we want to see ourselves, but our true reason for being this way isn't known to us. Here I'm not talking about the false, protective mask that we're aware we have with others. Here we're talking about the mask we wear with ourselves. This mask is much more difficult to see and sometimes takes a lot of work to see. This is because this mask is often created as a way of helping us deal with the world. It's often learned when we're young and comes from family patterns (software) about how we should be.

Often these patterns aren't spoken but are unconscious messages we received from our family about how to get our needs met. This is why I say they are deep. Think about the type of person that we want others to think that we are. Maybe it's a kind and caring person. Maybe it's an independent person who doesn't need anyone. Maybe it's the tough, in control person. It might even be the helpless female. How conscious are we of the mask that we're showing to others that says, "This is who I really am"?

Once I was back in my home town to go to a high school class reunion. Several of my high school friends decided to get together the night before. There was one woman there who I'd known since the third grade and who was sitting across the table from me. At one point I looked at her, smiled, and jokingly said, "So you're playing lawyer." She became angry and in an angry and firm tone of voice said, "I AM a lawyer!" I then smiled and in a friendly, relaxed way said, "I've been playing psychotherapist for years. It makes life much more fun when we don't take it all so seriously." There was little conversation between us after that. This was a woman I had played games with, played house with, and played many of the other childhood activities that children enjoy. It never occurred to me that she would be so upset by a simple, joking statement like I made. Later another friend said she complained about me "being in her face." Think about this situation. What was so threatening to this woman that she became so upset by this simple, what I thought was playful, statement, especially to such a point that she held onto her anger and later talked about me to our other friends? If I guessed, I would think it was because her deeper mask was connected to being a lawyer somehow. Obviously, she was very threatened by this simple statement. Think about it. When we were growing up it seemed that it was important to this woman to be smart. Maybe this was connected to her lawyer mask. After all, lawyers have to be pretty smart. Right? Because I've never asked her about it, I can only guess about what may have been going on; but there was no doubt that I had threatened her in some way.

Some people in the helping professions say that if we want to become a certain way, then we start by acting that way. There is some truth in acting the way we want to become. Maybe it is pretending at the start, but after time it can become more of who or how we really are. I'm not talking here, though, about what we want to become. I'm talking more about how we think we are. Maybe we see ourselves as a kind and caring person and often put ourselves out for others. Why do we do this? Do we do it for the pure desire to help others, or do we do it because we want others to see and believe that we're a good person who helps others? Deep down, do we do it because by helping others they come to need us? If people need us, then in some way we have control. They'll give us control to keep us around. If we have control we don't have to worry about people leaving or hurting us. After all, they need us. I know this one very well as I have already described. I was sad when I started to see the pollution in my helping of others. This pollution didn't make me a bad person. It was just the mask I had created to get what I thought I needed. It was a mask that I created to get attention and love from my father and others after my mother's death. There was a huge freedom that I felt when

I discovered and let go of this mask. When I help others now it's more pure and the desire is to help them, not to be in control and help, protect, or support myself. The joy I have from helping others is much greater now that the polluted desire has been revealed and is gone.

The fact that a mask is a deep one can make it threatening to see. For example, in the past in my private practice I taught a class called Chi Gong (Qigong). Chi Gong is a set of physical exercises created by someone in China as a way to stay healthy. One time at the start of a new class, a group of women who worked together came to take the class. There were four or five of them. The woman who contacted me about them coming to the class said she was happy that she found this class that they could all take together. One of these women was older than the rest and seemed to be one of influence with them. She seemed to be some type of leader. One day before class I was talking to this woman about the idea of people wearing a mask to the world. In the next class this woman, the leader, told me, "I thought about what you said, and I don't think I wear a mask." I said that this was really great and that the next step was to see the mask that we wear with ourselves. This woman seemed very irritated by what I said and didn't say good-bye when they left. None of these women returned to class after that day. The woman who had first contacted me called to say they would not be returning to the class. Her voice sounded sad and she didn't seem to have or to know a reason for why they weren't returning. Later, as I thought about why these women had decided not to return to the class, I wondered if the woman in the position of power, the leader, was threatened by the idea of seeing the mask she wore with herself. She certainly didn't like the idea when I brought it up. I wondered if she chose to not return and the others followed. After all, they previously had all been excited and willing to come and had already come to three classes. There seemed to be no other explanation. Of course, because I couldn't directly ask "the leader" about this, I can't say this for certain.

I have heard the Dalai Lama say that if we are going to be selfish, to be wise selfish. So what does this mean? Well, wise selfishness is helping others because it helps us. What we get out of this type of helping is a good feeling about ourselves. If we aren't aware that we're helping others because we get something out of it, though, it's just another mask. This is a mask that people wear with themselves at times. It can be this kind, loving, self-sacrificing person mask. There are many people in the helping professions or who are helping others in general, who aren't aware that they're really helping others to feel good about themselves. They're often so wrapped up in the mask they wear with themselves ("See what a good person I am?") that they are afraid to look at it. It's such a part of their self-esteem or how they control their world, that to look at it is too frightening. I'm not saying this is bad. I'm saying that the only way to begin to honestly help and care about others is to see and deal with this mask. Only then can we begin to honestly care about others, not for us but for them. The good feelings we get are a bonus, not the reason for doing it. There are, of course, many choices that people make that aren't about feeling good about themselves by helping others. This is just one mask well known to me, and one that I've seen a lot in my professional and spiritual experiences with others.

3) We believe people's masks are how and who they really are.

One day a friend of mine was at my house helping me understand how to use my video camera. This friend was someone who people saw as a healer and spiritual teacher. They believed this about her because this is who she presented herself to be. On this day we were just talking casually about this book and the idea of people's masks. I was surprised when she calmly said, "I never show people how I really am." Her tone of voice was very serious and I knew she was telling the truth. She didn't say more and I didn't press her, so I didn't threaten her. From our conversation, though, she was telling me that people didn't really know her but only knew her mask. After all, how could we possibly know her if she "never" showed people how she really was? As I watched her in the future it was clear that her self-esteem was caught up in, and depended on, others seeing her as really being her healer, spiritual teacher mask. I saw her look upset on more than one occasion when someone didn't seem to see her as this type of person.

> **LET'S STOP FOR A MINUTE. Let's think about this.** *My friend said she never showed people how she really was, so who was this healer and spiritual teacher she was showing others? Why did she get upset when someone didn't seem to see her this way? What was so threatening about this?* **Stop now and think WHIGO?** *Do you think*

she would have been upset with others if this was who she really was? **But** *what about you? Have you ever been upset when someone didn't believe what you wanted them to believe about you? Do you think you might wear a mask with yourself? Has this mask or view of yourself helped you or caused you suffering?*

On another occasion I was with some friends who were friends with a well-known spiritual teacher in the area where we lived. One day we went to one of her classes. After the class we went home with her and were sitting around talking. I remember her making fun of some of the people and some of the questions they asked her during the class. I remember being shocked to hear her making fun of people because she was thought of as such a loving and nonjudgmental person. This was certainly not what she showed us in private.

A German woman I worked with in Asia said to me, "Americans are so insecure." She didn't explain what she meant, and I didn't ask questions because of how negative she was being. This was a statement that I had heard people from other countries say several times before. I was at lunch once with a woman from Australia and a man from England. The man said, "I think Americans are insecure because they don't have a queen." This statement sent the Australian woman into a very irritated reply about Australians not having a queen and not being insecure. From my side, though, I had long before decided to keep quiet about "Americans are this or that" statements because I saw no purpose in having such conversations. I decided, though, that when I returned to America to work in the summer, I would watch for signs of Americans' insecurity.

I would watch to see if I could see something that might be causing people to believe this way.

On my return to America, I started to watch for what might be causing people from other countries to think that Americans are insecure. I came to understand that America is a country where we can never be successful enough, thin enough, attractive enough, accomplished enough, *enough*. There is a constant comparison with others that seem thinner, richer, smarter, more accomplished, and on and on. This message comes from the television, magazines, advertisements, and so forth. We'll even find it in casual conversations as people compare themselves with others. This culture drives an impossible effort to be perfect with the message that perfection is possible. If we get no other message, we get that we are less. This message in itself steps on our self-esteem, how we feel about ourselves. I remember telling a young Australian woman I knew who was coming to America to work to be aware that Americans "have very powerful masks." I explained to her that Americans were very good at showing themselves as secure and "all together." I think this powerful mask is a response to this constant comparison to others, and the impossible desire for perfection that we're told is possible. This mask is often the more superficial mask that we are aware of, but can also be part of the deeper mask. I remember when the actress Jamie Lee Curtis came out to the world and told women about the touch ups done on her pictures, in her movies, and so forth that showed her as having a perfect body. I admired her for telling women that it just wasn't true. This is one less, unreachable goal of perfection for American women to strive to achieve.

After being overweight and teased for two years in grade school, I became thin and began to get a lot of positive attention. People started telling me I was pretty. Being thin, and all the resulting attention it gave me, became very important to me; but I wasn't aware of it. It was so important that the summer before my senior year of high school I made myself sick through dieting, so sick that I fainted at work and was taken to the hospital. It was lucky for me that this happened, because it scared me into not doing extreme dieting. Years later when my weight was normal, I saw an old boyfriend from high school. He said to me, "What happened to you? You were so pretty before." What would have happened if I'd married him, considering that I was now no longer extremely thin? No one was aware that my very thin, pretty girl mask was actually a source of suffering. It required me to almost starve myself.

On one occasion when I was in college, I was with some friends from home and some of their friends. They were playing cards when one of these girls I didn't know looked at me and said, "Look at you. You're so full of yourself. You think you're something." I was very surprised and said, "I'm feeling insecure. That's why I'm sitting here quietly. I don't know you. You don't know me. I get quiet when I feel insecure."

LET'S STOP FOR A MINUTE. Let's think about this. *We've just been talking about several examples where people thought something different about people than they really were. Do you think that people usually show us how they really think or feel?* **Stop now and think. WHIGO?** *Is it possible that people aren't how or who they're showing themselves to be?* **But** *what about you?*

Do you show and tell people how you really think and feel? Do you wear a mask to hide something about yourself? Has wearing a mask helped you or caused you suffering? Have you ever thought someone was a certain way, only to find out differently?

How many of us show people how we really feel and see ourselves to be? Do we tell and show people when we're feeling insecure? Do we tell someone when we feel hurt by something they've done? I'm not talking about getting angry and yelling or anything like that. I'm asking if we speak up and tell the person that we feel hurt. When we're feeling hurt, and we express it in the form of anger, this anger is just another piece of the mask, a protection. We might say that when we're hurt, we are angry. Well this is true for a lot of people. This anger is a learned protection behavior, though, an automatic thought-feeling response pattern. Not everyone responds with anger. Here, though, I'm talking about being "for real," being aware of and showing or talking about our real feelings. Of course this is difficult to do if we haven't become aware of the masks we wear with ourselves. We may honestly believe we're angry, but hurt is often behind the fear and anger. This is the fight (angry) or flight (fear) response that even animals use: the instinct to survive. What is there to survive, though?

Have you ever had a conversation with someone after you've gotten to know them better, only to find out that they don't really feel inside what they've been saying and showing? One of the most surprising topics through which this happened to me was sex. I got married in 1976 at the age of twenty-two. This was the time when the sexual revolution for American women was at its peak. I had more than one friend talking about exploring their sexuality. I often wondered if there was something wrong with me because I didn't think I would be comfortable with having casual sex partners. I remember thinking, "What's wrong with me?" when I heard these female friends boast about their experiences. Years later, several of them confessed that they were really just looking for love. Of course, I was very surprised when I learned the truth, when they told me that this wasn't a positive experience for them. This is an example of how people will tell us one thing to create an image of themselves, yet they know that this image isn't true.

We've already talked about the mask of the person who tries to show themselves as very intelligent to hide the feeling of being less than others. There are masks that people wear that seem similar, but in reality each individual has their own mask. There are as many masks as there are people who wear them. Masks are used to try to increase and protect our self-esteem through getting people, and ourselves, to believe what we want them to believe about us. Because of this, each person will have their own specific mask that comes from their specific, inner programs.

4) We're all doing the best we can for where we are at the time. We're all just doing what we think we need to do to be okay.

How many of us do things because we want to harm ourselves? Even the people who deliberately cut themselves will tell us they do it to try to feel better. This is a common response that I've heard from people who cut on themselves. Whether it feels like a release, makes them feel alive, or is a punishment they think they deserve, it's *always* about the desire to feel better. They continue to hurt themselves because it relieves their anxiety. Some people's anxiety is so high that I have heard them say it's like "I bleed, therefore I am." Cutting somehow makes them feel better, at least in their minds. Most of us don't go to this extreme to feel better about ourselves and our world, but it's easy for us all to understand choosing an action that we believe will make us feel better. For most of us, cutting ourselves wouldn't work. It would make us feel worse; but does that mean that the person who cuts on themselves is bad, crazy, or sadistic? No, none of these judgements is true. It just makes them people who have learned unhealthy behaviors for dealing with their anxiety and feelings and the world around them. They can, and often do, learn to change this behavior and replace it with healthier ways of relieving their anxiety and expressing themselves.

We're all the result of our experiences (software) and mind (our genes that created our hard drive). We all would be healthy, happy, and pain free if we had our choice. We're where we are because of the life that we've lived so far. If we don't like where or what we are, then we can change it. One might say we can't change. Well, we can all look back on our lives and see how we've made changes. I'm not saying that it's easy, but it's truly possible. The key is to look at where we are now, accept it, and begin to see what we want to change and what we want to keep and strengthen. For every person in whom we can see a negative, I can guarantee there is also positive. This is the case for all of us. We're all trying to be something. Until we are God, Buddha, or whatever higher being we believe in, if that's possible, then we're all developing. We're a work in progress, and this is okay. *This is human.* Bottom line, we're all just trying to be happy.

5) We're all just making choices that we believe will make us happy.

We all make choices because we get something from it. If we don't get something from it, we don't do it. Remember talking about the Dalai Lama saying, "If you are going to be selfish be wise selfish." What does this statement mean? This statement is about doing something for ourselves by doing something for others. If it feels good to help others, if it helps us to be happy, then help others. Remember, though, that in reality we're doing it for us not them. We get something from it or we wouldn't do it. Here, it's the good feeling about ourselves or the good feeling of seeing someone else feel better, but it's about how we feel. It's wise selfishness because it's helpful to others and is helpful to us.

LET'S STOP FOR A MINUTE. Let's think about this. *We only make choices because we get something from it, and that something is about happiness.* **Stop now and think. WHIGO?** *Think about this idea that all our choices are about being happy. Think about this idea of wise selfishness;* **but** *what about you? Have you ever made a choice to do something that you weren't happy about? What was this choice about? If you look closely, was even this choice about making yourself happy in* *some way, even if it was only to please your boss, someone in your family, or something similar? Bottom line, if you look closely, why do you think you make the choices you do in your life?*

In Secret Feelings number six (We all want to be happy) we talked about how we make our choices because we want happiness. Many people see money as a major path to happiness. Because of this belief, they put out a lot of effort to get money, legally and illegally. Whigo? Why is this? It's not the paper that makes us happy, but what we can get with the paper, money. We work to get money, so we can get the objects we think will make us happy.

A common, mistaken-belief that people have is that we need a particular person in our life to be happy. Suppose a woman leaves her boyfriend for another man. The boyfriend thinks that he can't be happy without her, so he begins to try to get her back. Maybe he sends her presents, calls her often, or follows her around hoping she will come back to him. This hope is decreased if she gets a new boyfriend. Being upset by this, he might start to do negative behaviors like cutting their car tires. Will this get him back with his old girlfriend? Probably not, as it will just scare her. Whigo? What is this thinking that causes us to believe we must have a certain person in our lives? This is usually about looking to this other person for happiness. Is it true that someone else can make us happy? How many people do we know who were happy in a relationship and then later were unhappy in the relationship with this same person? If someone could make us happy, that wouldn't change with time.

We make small choices every day with our happiness

in mind. Most of the time, though, we don't know that happiness is the reason behind our choices. Getting to know ourselves and the reasons we make choices will help us find the happiness that we want. It'll just not be found using the usual things, outside objects, people, accomplishments, and so on, that we have come to believe are the way to success. Lasting, stable happiness can't be found outside of us. It can only be found through an inner path. By becoming aware of our choices, why we make them, and how we are using them to try to be happy, we can continue to make these choices, or different choices if needed. We'll then be closer to the lasting, stable happiness we seek.

6) Resisting looking at ourselves will only increase our suffering, not make it go away.

While attending a play with some friends, I went up to one of my male friends during the intermission and flirted with him. His response was something I would have expected from someone much younger. I laughed and said, "Isn't it interesting how our bodies are older, but we can still be that teenager inside." He understood and agreed. Think of the times when we've heard a song, seen something in a movie, or heard something on television which brought back a memory. If there are strong feelings connected to the memory, we can feel like we're right there in the same situation again. I can't tell anyone how to totally remove a memory from their mind. I can tell you, though, how to let go of the strong feelings that give the memory power and cause it to continue to affect our experiences.

It's the strong feelings that are causing the memory to affect us each day. It's the strong feelings that keep the memory as a software program on our hard drive. "What we resist, persists." If it's an inner software program on our hard drive, it will continue to affect how we see situations, how we feel, and the choices we make in our life, until we become aware of it. How to stop the programs from affecting our life so much is discussed in depth in the answers section.

> **LET'S STOP FOR A MINUTE. Let's think about this.** *Is it possible that something that happened to us when we were very young could still be affecting us when we're much older? Can we really feel like we're back in a past situation just by remembering the feelings we had then?* **Stop now and think. WHIGO?** *Think about this idea that a past event that we had strong feelings about can affect us in the present day moment;* **but** *what about you? Have you ever been going about your day and something happened to take you back to an old memory or event? Did the feelings make it seem like you were re-experiencing this same or a similar experience? What type of software program do you think might be involved here?*

Once when I was visiting in my home town, I spent an evening with several of the women I grew up with. We were in our late thirties at the time. At one point several of the women said they wanted to leave the house we were at to go have drinks. We all then started talking about who was going to go. The women I was still close to and trusted were not going to go. One of the women who planned to go was Kathy, the girl who was unkind to me the day my mother died. I tried to get one of my close friends to come along. She said to me, "How is it that you can travel the world and still be uncomfortable going for drinks with these women?" I thought about this and realized it was because I still had this mistrust, and thereby fear, of Kathy. I wasn't insecure with Kathy; I just wasn't comfortable being with her without my normal supports in this group. I still saw her as someone who I couldn't trust and who might try to harm me in some way. I was right back there in those old eleven-year-old-girl feelings.

Many times I have heard people express a fear that they're going to lose control, that they can't take something anymore. I often then discuss this idea of "I can't take it anymore" by using a comparison between us and a pressure cooker or tea kettle. With a pressure cooker or tea kettle, there's a pressure that builds up until steam is released, which results in a whistling sound. Our stuffing or holding in of emotions in our body is like what happens in the cooker or kettle. We can only hold in so much before the pressure, stress, builds up and the steam is ready to be released. It's this pressure that people feel that makes them think they're going to lose control. The issue isn't really one of being about to lose control, but one of being in a place where there's no more room to stuff or hold in our feelings, where the pressure needs to be released. The human body has a built-in physical release value for letting off steam: tears. When we cry, a stress hormone, adrenocorticotropin, is released, which helps us to relax. If we don't allow ourselves to cry, the pressure will continue to build and build until we feel we can no longer hold in our feelings. Some people experience this as feeling like they're going to lose control. The problem isn't one of losing control, but one of being too controlled.

I try regularly to get people to understand the problems created by the mistaken belief that there's something wrong with crying, that it's a weakness or whatever word we choose to put on it because of our software programs. How could crying be wrong if it's the physical release built into the body? It doesn't make sense, but it's a strong misunderstanding, mistaken belief, or cultural program in many Western cultures. I say Western because I haven't seen this in many Eastern cultures. We need to let ourselves cry, be human, and let our natural body functions take care of our mental, emotional, and physical needs. I try to help people understand that if our culture says it is a weakness to cry, that it really takes a lot of strength and courage to go against this incorrect, mistaken belief and let ourselves cry. Be strong for yourself! Don't resist so it persists. If crying is difficult for us to start with, then there are other ways of releasing emotions that we will talk about in the answers section. Crying is just the simplest, most healthy one that is built into our body.

7) No one can make us think, feel, say, or do anything.

The most amazing examples of this secret are some of the Tibetan Buddhist Lamas, monks, and nuns who have been held and tortured in Chinese prisons. I have had the privilege of meeting Lamas (the Tibetan word for teacher) who talk about meditating on compassion for the people who tortured them. They talk about having compassion for the person doing the torture. This is because they see the Chinese person torturing them as creating negative karma which will cause them to suffer in the future. These people are truly amazing. Often they seem to have a light and peacefulness in them that I have rarely encountered elsewhere. This is an example of how someone can take control of us physically, but they can't control our arms, legs, thoughts, and so on to *make us* do something.

Any type of prisoner is an example of someone taking physical control over someone else, whether that is a prisoner of war or in jail. In both these situations the person has been forced to be in a particular place, *but* they weren't forced to walk there. We might say this isn't true. If the prisoner hadn't walked there, they would have been picked up and carried or beaten. These two things are the results of the prisoner making the choice to not go along with walking to a certain place. To do as we are requested to do is a choice, a choice which avoids certain results. If we choose to avoid certain results, it's just that: *a choice*. Most of us would make a similar choice to avoid unpleasant results, but it's a choice. Prisoners are just great examples of people who have had someone take physical control over them. They would probably be the first to admit, though, that the ones who control them physically, in some way, don't have control over their thoughts, feelings, and choices. Prisoners of war have told stories about using such things as mental exercises and games to help them keep their minds and feelings up in spite of their horrible situation. There are also stories of prisoners being tortured to get information from them. Many of these prisoners choose to take the result of torture over giving information. This is a real example of how someone can't control what we think, feel, say, or do.

> **LET'S STOP FOR A MINUTE. Let's think about this.** *Is it true that someone can only control us physically? It seems like people can make us feel certain ways. Is this true in reality?* **Stop now and think. WHIGO?** *Think about whether someone else can really control us;* **but** *what about you? Have you ever thought that you didn't have a choice about how you thought or felt about something? Were you aware that you could make different choices? Do you think you were coming from an automatic thought-feeling program? Have you ever tried to make someone else think, feel, or do something and were unsuccessful? Why was this?*

Think of the different things our parents or others have tried to get us to think, feel, say, or do. Sometimes they're successful, sometimes not. Let's take for example when someone calls us an unpleasant name. At this time, we have several ways in which we can respond. We can get angry, we can cry, we can walk away hurt, we can think, "This person doesn't know me, so they have no knowledge on which to make this statement," and on and on are our choices. Our choices for responding are limited only by us. One might say, "Well, if someone calls me a name, I immediately feel angry or hurt. I don't think about it, it just happens." This is what we talked about in Secret Thoughts numbers two and three, where we talked about how we are programed and how automatic thought-feeling patterns are created. We all have created patterns of thinking, feeling, and behaving from our experiences growing up. If anger is okay in our family and showing that we're vulnerable isn't, then we'll probably respond with anger. If anger wasn't okay in our family, then we'll respond with what our family has taught us is the correct way to respond. Just because we've developed an emotional or automatic thought-feeling pattern doesn't mean we haven't made a choice. It only means that we have a habit (automatic thought-feeling pattern) to respond in this way and that we're not aware of the thoughts that happen before our feelings. We're not aware we have actually made a choice.

In the 1950s, Albert Ellis created a type of therapy that he called Rational Emotive Therapy (now called Rational Emotive Behavioral Therapy, REBT) (Ellis and Harper 1997). REBT is like the grandparent to current cognitive therapies like Dialectic Behavioral Therapy (DBT) and Cognitive Behavioral Therapy (CBT). Such therapies center on changing how we think in order to change how we feel. They're about helping us understand that only we have control over our thoughts, and thereby our feelings, and that it's up to us to make changes if we want to feel differently. They center on gaining insight into just what our thoughts are, with the idea that feelings come from thoughts. If we change the thought, then we can change how we feel.

If someone else could really control how we think or feel, I would have already set about the world making everyone understand how special they are and making everyone happy. Wouldn't that be awesome? Even though it's not possible, that doesn't mean that I didn't try to do this with people in the past. I found out, though, that I was only successful when they chose to believe me.

8) We're in control of what we think, feel, say, and do.

Once while I was working on a psychiatric inpatient unit, a female patient, whom I had never seen before, approached me as I was handing out medications. She was very angry and said to me, "You look like shit." I looked at her, smiled, and said, "Thank you very much." Her facial expression was one of surprise, and she turned and walked away. If I had tried to defend myself, chances are she would have gotten angrier. As it was, she had no one to argue with, and she walked away. Later that same evening I had several co-workers come up to me and ask how I was able to react in such a way. My answer to them was, "Why would I react differently? I obviously don't look like shit. What would be the point of responding differently? It wasn't personal, even though it may have seemed that way to you." The main thought in my mind when I was answering these co-workers was, "Why would you have responded differently?" Part of a psychiatric professional's job is to not take the behavior of clients personally.

> **LET'S STOP FOR A MINUTE. Let's think about this.** *Is it possible to learn that anyone's response towards us isn't personal? It's one thing to do it with clients, but what about peers, friends, family, and so on? After all, they know us personally, and so they may be making their comments personal. Is it possible to still not take it personally?* **Stop now and think. WHIGO?** *If we are in control of what we think, feel, say, or do, is it possible to not feel that things are personal?* **But** *what about you? Have you ever had someone say something negative about or to you, and you had an automatic reaction to*

it? How did you feel? Did you feel strong with this response or more upset? Have you ever had someone try to upset you, and you chose not to get upset? How did this make you feel? Did you feel strong or more upset?

Being aware of ourselves and how we're feeling at the time something happens is powerful. This awareness is important to help us stop and realize that we can choose how we react in any situation, that we're the ones in control of our thought, feeling, and behavioral choices. No one can make us think, feel, say, or do anything. It's our choice because we're the ones with the controls. Choosing not to respond with an automatic thought-feeling pattern in a situation helps us keep our personal power. Not only do we not experience the helplessness that comes with blaming others and responding from automatic patterns, but we also feel strong, in control, and even powerful. It's awesome. This is made easier when we remember that anyone's response towards us comes from their clouded view programs and not from a true view of us. So why would we take responsibility for and believe their clouded view of us?

This secret may seem a repetition of Secret Behavior number seven, no one can make us think, feel, say, or do anything. I promise, though, that even with all the possible ways that I can think of to introduce someone to this reality, still our mistaken beliefs (software programs that are so firmly on our hard drive) will try to make us not believe it. Again, one of the greatest mistaken beliefs that people have is about our automatic feelings (automatic thought-feeling patterns). People will point out that they thought or felt a certain way without thinking about it first. Habits, automatic thought-feeling patterns, are created very young and can seem automatic. If we look at ourselves five, ten, or twenty years ago, were we the same then as now? Have we made any changes? If the answer is yes, then we can understand that we have changed. Patterns or habits, whether thought, feeling, or behavioral, can be changed.

Think of an adult male that got into fights when he was a teenager but doesn't now. As an adult male if he would get into a fight he runs a greater risk of being charged with assault. The result of fighting could be jail. This possible result can be enough for him to change his adolescent pattern of fighting. Most men would choose to walk away from a fight for this reason, unless it's self-defense. Self-defense is still a choice but not really what we're talking about here. He may have changed his behavioral choice, but has his automatic thought-feeling pattern changed? We'll look at this more in depth in the answers chapter.

Just as we continue to choose to behave in certain ways because we get something out of it, we often choose to blame others for our thoughts, feelings, and behaviors, trying to feel okay about ourselves. This is a very common behavior. After all, many of society's messages strengthen this thinking. The biggest problem with choosing to blame others is that it makes us feel helpless. After all, if someone made us think, feel, or behave in a certain way, then they have power over us. We may feel good telling ourselves we aren't responsible, but by believing this we have given our control and power over to them and set ourselves up to feel helpless.

As a therapist I have often heard kids talk about

wanting to do something to someone who has hurt them. Very often the person, who they're upset with, wanted to upset them. I talked with the kids about whether they wanted to give their power and control over to this person by choosing to be upset, giving that person what they wanted, or did they want to make a different choice about what to think and feel and how to behave. Did they want to keep their power? It's always a decision to make. If we blame others, we give them our power and feel helpless like we have no choice or control. How can this blaming create anything but suffering? Often we will go over an unpleasant situation in our mind and wonder what we should have said or done, or what to do in the future. Is this a pleasant experience? Usually it isn't.

If we take responsibility for ourselves, which is the true reality, then we keep our own personal power and decrease, and in time eliminate, our sense of helplessness. We don't have to choose to go over and over something in our mind. We can choose to just let it go. By letting it go we take back our power. It's at these times that we can be clear about how we might want to behave in the future with someone. After all, we're in control. Sometimes it's helpful to go over a situation if we can keep our unpleasant emotions out of it. What we think and feel, and how we behave is always about choices.

9) We can't make someone else think, feel, say, do, or be anything.

Often I've heard people say that they believe they can make someone else happy. One young girl I worked with said she knew she could make her mother happy. As we talked, I asked her if there was ever a time when she tried to make her mother happy, and it didn't work. She said yes, but most of the time she was able to. She said she knew what her mother liked and would do these things when her mother was down, in an attempt to make her happy. Most of the time it worked. What about those times that it didn't work?

> **LET'S STOP FOR A MINUTE. Let's think about this.** *This girl thought she really had the power to "make" her mother feel a certain way. If she was really able to control and "make" her mother feel a certain way, then wouldn't it have worked every time?* **Stop now and think. WHIGO?** *If we have the power to make someone think, feel, do, or be something, then why aren't we successful every time?* **But** *what about you? Have you ever tried to make someone think, feel, do, or be something and you were successful? Have you ever tried to make someone think, feel, do, or be something and you were unsuccessful? Why is it that it worked sometimes and didn't other times?*

Think about all the times we've tried to get someone to think, feel, do, or be something. Think of the times that we wanted someone to love or like us and they didn't. Why didn't they love or like us? We must have tried to make this happen. If one has children, especially teenagers, think of how many times we've tried to get our child to do or become something, and it didn't work. Look at all the times we tried to get our parents to think, feel, or believe something, and they didn't. An even more powerful relationship where we often try to have control is with our partner. We want them to think, feel, do, or be certain ways all the time. Many times it doesn't work. If we begin to look, it's easy to see that it isn't possible to control someone else. With a small child we can pick them up and take them to their room if they don't do what we want (this physical control we discussed before). Even then, if the child refuses to stay in their room, the only way to make them stay is to hold them down or lock them in.

Most of us have tried to make someone feel a certain way whether that is happy, hurt, angry, or so on. If we put a lot of energy into trying to get someone to feel a certain way, and it works, then I think we have a very small amount of responsibility for what they feel because we tried so hard to create these feelings in them. We can really only be successful, though, if they allow us to be. This is why I say a very small amount of responsibility because they're really the ones in control of whether they're going to feel a certain way. Remember the story about the woman telling me I looked like shit? I'm sure the reaction that she wanted from me wasn't the smile and thank you that she got.

It's very important, if we're going to use the tools that I am talking about here, that we understand that we can't control others. It's also very important to understand that we can only make someone think, feel, do, or be something if they agree to it. Yes, it's true that some people know our buttons to push, our automatic reactions (automatic thought-feeling patterns), because they know us or maybe because they were involved in our early programming. If we weren't able to control how we think, feel, or behave, though, we would never be able to change our patterns of reacting that were created at a young age. Someone can push our button (a button being an automatic thought-feeling pattern), but we're in control of whether or not it works to get the programmed response they're used to seeing in us. This doesn't mean that the automatic thought-feeling pattern won't come up. It may come up, but we can choose to go with it or not. In order to choose not to go with an automatic thought-feeling pattern, we must first be able to see that the automatic pattern is there. We must come to know what our patterns are. In the answers chapter we'll discuss how to do the work so that unwanted patterns don't arise at all at some point.

10) We're not responsible for what others think, feel, say, or do.

There was a man I worked with who would often say to me, "I'm going to have to get a flannel shirt." Sometimes when he said this I was wearing a flannel shirt, sometimes not. Either way, I found this comment strange. One day another co-worker told me she wanted to know what I might want for Christmas because she was helping the co-worker who had picked my name in our gift exchange. She laughed and said that they thought about getting me a flannel shirt, and added, "You know you're known for them." Surprised, I told her I found this strange because I only owned two flannel shirts, so I had no idea why someone would think this. Later I was working with this same woman and the man who always talked about flannel shirts with me. It seems that this man was the one talking about me always wearing flannel shirts. He had to admit, though, that there wasn't any truth in his thinking when he understood I only owned two flannel shirts.

> **LET'S STOP FOR A MINUTE. Let's think about this.** *Someone thought something about me, that I always wore flannel shirts, that wasn't true in reality. How is it that this man came to think this about me?* **Stop now and think. WHIGO?** *If this man had been mistaken about such a simple thing, how many other things about me and others might he be mistaken about?* ***But*** *what about you? Have you ever thought something about someone and later found out it wasn't true? Has anyone ever thought something about you, and you later showed them that it wasn't true? Who's responsible for what we and others think about someone or something?*

In Secret Behaviors numbers seven through nine, we've talked about how no one can make us think, feel, say, or do anything; that we're in control of what we think, feel, say, and do, and that we can't make someone else think, feel, say, do, or be anything. If this is true, then how can we possibly be responsible for what others think, feel, say, and so on? Think about it for a moment. How can we be responsible for someone or something that we can't control? We can *choose* to take responsibility for others, but this is a choice and a mistaken belief. If we can't control someone or something, then we aren't responsible. In order to be responsible for someone else, a situation, and so on, we must have the control to decide how everything will go.

There was a woman I worked with named Sue who would easily become upset with people. When I was the one she was upset with, I would tell her that this wasn't how I wanted her to feel, and that I would never do anything on purpose to upset her. As much as I tried to help her see that I didn't want her to feel this way, that I didn't try to make her feel this way, and that she was the only one who was in control, I was never able to get her to change how she saw situations. I would tell her that if I was in control, and by this responsible for how she felt, she wouldn't feel the way she did.

Think of the situations where a parent is contacted because of something their child has done. I'm sure everyone can identify with the parent's reply, "I can't control him/her." Several USA state governments have talked about making laws to hold parents partly responsible for the actions of their children in certain situations. I know that the courts are very aware that the parent wasn't in control of the child. The governments are asking the parents to accept responsibility for making it easy for the child to commit the crime. This might be about making a gun available to the child, so that it's easy for the child to do the illegal act. The child is not set fee. The court understands that the child was responsible for doing the act. The parents are seen as something like accessories to the crime. Here I'm talking about situations were a child is able to get a gun from home and do some harm. It may be a situation where a child isn't supervised or is neglected to the point that the parent isn't aware of or doesn't care about what the child is doing. This isn't really what we are talking about here, but it needs to be talked about because it's about being responsible for others. The parent didn't force the child to do the act, so they aren't responsible for the child's actions. They are responsible for their own actions, though, whether that is keeping a gun in a place easy for someone to get to or being so wrapped up in other things that they don't pay enough attention to or get help for their child. I'm not judging the parents here. I'm just talking about responsibility for others.

As I said before, if we try very hard to get someone to think, feel, or do something, and it works, then we share a very, very small amount, maybe one percent, of the responsibility because of the large amount of energy we put into making it happen. In reality, though, that person is in control of the functions of their body which includes the use of their vocal cords. They could say no. *If we don't have control, we aren't responsible.* This is because if we aren't in control, we aren't making the decisions and choices about how someone thinks, feels, or behaves. Think about all the times we wanted someone to think, feel, say, or do something, and it didn't work. How can we then be responsible? If we wanted our partner to be happy about something we said or did, and they weren't, how can we be responsible for this? We tried, so how can we be responsible? If we had control over our partner, they would think, feel, or be what we wanted because we could control them. We would then be responsible. If they aren't responding the way we want that's because we can't control them, so we aren't responsible for however they choose to think, feel, or be, even if they try to say we are.

11) Others aren't responsible for what we think, feel, say, or do.

We just talked in Secret Behavior number ten about how we aren't responsible for what others think, feel, say, or do. I've often tried to help others feel better by helping them understand that they're in control of and responsible for what they think, feel, say, or do. I talk about how I don't take responsibility for others because I can't control them, and that because others can't control me, I don't hold them responsible for what I think, feel, or do. I choose to keep my power and decide how I want to think or feel.

> **LET'S STOP FOR A MINUTE. Let's think about this.** *Do we give our power away to others when we hold them responsible for what we think, feel, or do?* **Stop now and think. WHIGO?** *If I take responsibility for my choices do I feel more powerful?* **But** *what about you? Have you ever blamed someone for what you think, feel or do? How did you feel after blaming them? Were you feeling frustrated or helpless? Have you ever been in a situation where you took control and responsibility for your choices, even if someone was trying to get you to choose differently? How did you feel? Do you think there were any of your programs that came up? Did these choices help you or cause you suffering?*

Just as it's true that we aren't responsible for others, it's also true that they aren't responsible for us. If we say that others are responsible for us, we're saying they're in control of us in some way. If we believe this to be true, then we're powerless to do anything about it. If we take control and live in the reality of the truth, that we're the only ones who are in control of ourselves, then we take our power back. Once we begin to take our power back, then other things fall into place. We start to understand that because we're the ones in control, we can make different choices. Stop for a minute and think about something that might be different if we stopped blaming someone or something else and chose to do something different. I can still remember the power I felt as I began to live this truth.

In 1991 I returned from Asia because I was invited to work at a healing center in California. I left this job after a few months and returned to the area where my family was. At that time, I was close to developing chronic fatigue syndrome. This left me in a position where I didn't have the energy to stay in my normal pattern of taking emotional care of my friends and family. Some of my friends and certain members of my family seemed to become more distant from me. I was always there for them. Why weren't they being there for me?

After looking at this situation carefully I began to understand that I was blaming them for not being there for me and for my hurt feelings. The truth was, though, that I was the one who had changed the rules of our relationship, not them. So how was it that they were responsible for how I felt? They didn't do anything differently. I was the one no longer willing or able to take care of them. By seeing this I was able to take my power back. I understood that if I wanted to keep this pattern in my relationships then the result might be that when I wasn't able to take care of someone, they would go away. This was very powerful for me to see. It helped me gain insight into and change an unhealthy automatic thought-feeling pattern.

It also greatly increased my insight into the mask I wore to myself: this mask of being the kind, caretaker person who was always there for my friends because I "had it all together." The mask was exposed as really being about being in control and protecting myself. I now look at this situation as a great blessing. My relationships with others are much healthier now. My relationships are now with people who I don't have to take care of. This is because I'm no longer afraid to let others give to me. I'm no longer trying to control others in order to prevent myself from being hurt. I no longer need to take care of others, so that they don't leave me.

12) We can't control what others think of us.

When I was a teenager I tried to make all the "right" choices because I never wanted my father to disapprove of me or be upset with me. In truth, I was trying to get his love. Several of my friends' parents really liked me and would let their children do anything with me. Some of these same friends liked me. Others thought "you're too serious" and were uncomfortable with the fact that I wouldn't do some of the things that they did. So who was correct, the parents and the kids who liked me, or the kids who didn't like me because I was "too serious, straight, no fun"? In reality none of them were correct because they had no clue about what was going on inside of me, and why I made the choices I did. They judged me from what they saw and put through their own programs (software). They had no idea that I wanted my father's love so much that this desire was much more powerful than any peer pressure. I cared more about what my father thought than what they thought, so I tried to behave in a way that I thought would please him. How could they have known, though, why I acted as I did, if I didn't even know it then?

> **LET'S STOP FOR A MINUTE. Let's think about this.**
> *I tried very hard to control what my father thought about me. Why? Because I wanted his love. Is it possible that a child's desire for love from their parents can override the strong, teenage desire to be accepted by their peers, peer pressure?* **Stop now and think. WHIGO?** *Can we control what everyone thinks about us when they have different beliefs and desires?* **But** *what about you? Have you ever tried to control what others think about you by how you look (makeup, clothes, cars, and on and on), what you say, or what you do? Were there any programs involved with this behavior? Did these choices help you feel happy or increase your suffering in some way?*

Trying to get people to think a certain way about us is something that we often put a lot of energy into, whether we want someone to think we are cool, nice, pretty, and so on. Think of all the times we have tried to control what others thought about us and it didn't work. It didn't work because the power of choice is inside each of us and comes from our programs. Do you think Brad Pitt is attractive? Some people do, others don't. I don't. Who's right? Someone told me once not to use this example because most people think Brad Pitt is gorgeous. I don't see him as gorgeous, so in my mind it's a good example. We can easily see how our inner programs can be different from others. We see things outside of us through our programs, so we'll each see different things.

We've all had a situation where we tried to get someone to like us or think that we're cool or something, and it didn't work. We often blame ourselves, thinking, "Why don't they love me?" or "Why don't they like me?" The simple answer is that it's about something in their software programs. They don't love or like us because of something in their software programs that doesn't see us as someone to love or like. *It says something about their mind or programs. It says nothing about us.*

So now that the secrets are out, what are we to think now? What does it mean if we believe that we all share these human experiences? What does it mean that we all experience the world from on our own specific, learned programs? What does it mean that we aren't in control of, and therefore aren't responsible for, others reactions to us? What does it mean that others aren't in control of us, and therefore are not responsible for our reactions to them? Well, it means that we're not alone in our human experience. It means we're all in this together, this condition of human being. It means we're not really helpless in dealing with the world and others. It means we're in control of what we think, feel, and do. *Last and most important,* it means that, **"We create our own world."**

· PART THREE ·
SOME ANSWERS

I

Introduction

Remember the woman I worked with named Sue, who easily got upset with others? She most often got upset whenever she thought someone was being disrespectful to her. This behavior caused a lot of problems for her with the people she worked with. One day I was working with Sue, and she stopped me to talk about something. Our shift was about to be over, and I was rushing to finish some checks on my patients. When she stopped me I told her I needed just a few minutes to finish what I was doing, and then we could talk. She looked angry, said something I didn't hear, and stormed away. In less than five minutes I went to her and said, "Okay, so let's talk." She was so angry that she refused to talk to me. I said, "Obviously, I must have missed something. Let's just talk now." I wasn't upset about anything and had approached her in a calm, open way. She continued to refuse to talk to me.

The next time I worked with Sue, she started our shift refusing to look at or talk to me. After several hours of ignoring me, she came to me and said, "Aren't you going to talk to me?" I told her that I didn't come to talk to her because I didn't have any problems with her. She was the one who seemed upset, so I decided to let her talk to me if she wanted. She began to talk about how disrespectful I had been to her. I tried to tell her that I saw the situation very differently, but she didn't seem able to hear me. She just got more and more angry, talking about how disrespectful I had been. I repeatedly told her that I would never intentionally disrespect or harm her, but I don't think she heard what I was trying to say. It was only after I apologized that she calmed down. What I was really apologizing for was that she chose to think that I had been disrespectful and had become so upset. In my view I hadn't been and didn't really understand how she could have become so upset about a request from me to wait a few minutes to talk.

We create our own world. When I say, "we create our own world," I'm not talking about the world outside of us. I'm not talking about other people, objects, or the situations in the world. I'm talking about our responses to and our interactions with the world and others. I'm talking about the inner experience that we have from what we decide to think and feel about what we see outside of ourselves. This is where understanding the Secret Behaviors comes in. They help us to understand the truth that only we control our thoughts, feelings, and actions, so we are the only ones responsible for ourselves and the decisions we make about the world outside of us. My coworker, Sue, was repeatedly creating a world for herself where she was disrespected and being harmed in some way. From these thoughts she then chose to react with anger and to be aggressive or passive aggressive with others in some way. These choices caused her a lot of unhappiness and problems with others.

Remember in Secret Behaviors number seven (No one can make us think, feel, or do anything) when we talked about cognitive therapies. These therapies base themselves on the idea that if we want to change how we feel, we must first change how or what we think. These therapies only work if we understand that we have control over ourselves, and that we have the power to make changes. Remember the comparison I used between us and a computer (PART ONE, Chapter II: Lasting, Stable Happiness), with our body and brain being the hard drive and our life experiences being the software programs. This comparison was used to show how we each have our own, individual, specific programs on our hard drive (brain), made up of the programs we're born with (gene hardware) and the programs from our experiences (software). If we start to pull all these ideas together, we can see that it's through our specific programs, made up of our own specific thoughts and feelings, that we see the world. It's like we see the world through our specific filter. How could we not?

> **LET'S STOP FOR A MINUTE. Let's think about this.**
> *Do you think that Sue had some software program saying that if someone disrespects her then she is being harmed in some way? If she does, then naturally she would respond with a self-defense program. What do you think Sue's self-defensive program might be? It doesn't matter whether her program came from personal experience or was taught to her. It seems like she was probably reacting from an automatic thought-feeling program because she*

> reacted quickly in situations and didn't seem able to talk about whether her thinking was true. **Let's stop now and think. WHIGO?** Think about how Sue's program is causing her problems with her co-workers. Do you think Sue or anyone is happy when they feel angry or threatened? **But** what about you? Are you aware of any automatic reactions you have in certain situations? Have you ever stopped to question whether your thinking is true? Are any of your programs causing problems and suffering for you?

We're the ones in control of what we think and feel about the world around us. With this in mind, we can now understand that how we see anything comes from what's in our inner programs. Can we believe our automatic thought-feeling programs? We can now understand that we can choose and take back control over what we believe. It's our programs that affect what we see and understand to be true, but are our programs true? **WE create our own world.**

When I talk about we "create our own world." I'm not talking about disbelieving what we see, hear, smell, or feel with our body senses. I'm talking about what we think, see and understand about whatever we see, hear, smell, taste, or feel with our body senses. Let's take the simple situation of eating spinach. Some people like the taste, some don't. Who is right? When I was young I always thought that I hated spinach, but the truth was that I had never tried spinach. When I did taste it, I loved it. It's now one of my favorite foods. Can you see how our programs can cloud what we believe? Somewhere in one of my programs I had a belief that I didn't like spinach. Well, of course, this was a mistaken belief because I had never eaten spinach; and when I did, I loved it. This false information, mistaken belief, on one of my programs has now been replaced with true information. "Yeah," you say, "but what about the hard stuff?" What about thoughts and feelings about relationships and our interactions with the world? Well, it's very similar. If we've experienced or been told certain things about people and the world, we approach all people and our world initially with these programs. The question becomes one of whether or not these programs are made up of true, logical, realistic thoughts and feelings. It's probable that my co-worker Sue was taught or had some experience about people disrespecting her and how disrespect was harmful. This experience then became an automatic thought-feeling pattern that she used when interacting with the world.

In 1988 I traveled to Thailand. When I first arrived I decided to go to a ten-day retreat at a Buddhist monastery. I still had no idea what this Buddhist stuff was, but I decided to go because several people I met while traveling in Hong Kong and China had told me about it. During the retreat we all slept on straw mats on a wooden floor. We weren't allowed to talk or even look people in the eye because this was considered talking. We ate one meal a day, lunch, which was often hot and spicy Thai food. It was very hot and humid and there were many mosquitoes. We got up at dawn and meditated most of the day until the sun went down. So there I was at my first Buddhist meditation retreat with forty people whom I had never met. Because it had only been a few months since I had left my very comfortable American lifestyle, I suffered mentally and physically. I had no soft bed, no air conditioner, no way to escape the mosquitoes, no cold water, no showers, no foods I liked, plus I couldn't talk to or even look at people. I was tired, hot, hungry, and irritable.

Because I was searching for answers, I tried to take my mind off my suffering. I then started to concentrate on the other people in the retreat. Because of this I became very aware of how they acted and how they looked physically. By the end of the retreat I was sure that I had each person figured out and that I knew what type of person they were. To my total surprise, at the end of the retreat when I started talking with the others, *no one was even close to being what I had imagined them to be.* My beliefs about them were completely wrong. This experience was a huge lesson about how we create our beliefs about others from our own minds. I see this experience as such a blessing now, a slap in the face with this truth: a wakeup call. After all, we aren't talking about how I was wrong about just one person. I was wrong about forty people! In fact, I remember how I had looked at one woman, who I thought was American, and thought she was a bitch. She was American, a good guess from how she dressed, but when we talked I found her to be the nicest one of the group. This was more evidence to me about how I created my world from my own mind. I had to admit I was the real bitch, or at least the negative thoughts in my mind were.

> **LET'S STOP FOR A MINUTE. Let's think about this.**
> *With all the software programs I had on my hard drive, why did I respond in such a negative way? What do you think my automatic thought-feeling programs were? Were my software programs helping my suffering*

or causing my suffering? **Let's stop now and think. WHIGO?** *Think about my possible software programs;* ***but*** *what about you? Has there ever been a time when you thought something about someone, only to find out later that what you had thought was wrong? Think about what automatic thought-feeling programs you were using before you learned the truth. Were these programs causing you happiness or suffering?*

You see, in my situation at the Buddhist retreat, I was lacking the physical comforts I was used to, so I easily fell into my negative programs. Because I was tired, hot, hungry, and being eaten by mosquitoes, it isn't surprising to me that my mind became negative. I'm reinforcing how I was feeling because it's important to understand that when we're in situations where we're without our normal comforts, our minds can fall more easily into our negative programs. This can cause us to increase our suffering because we then start to put our negative thinking out onto the world, a world which we have no control over. We then see negativity around us and begin to feel uncomfortable or not safe. If we aren't aware of this, it also brings up the feeling of helplessness that comes with blaming the outside world for our thoughts and feelings. Such suffering, huh? I think we can now get a picture of what I have been saying.

Most of us never question the thoughts and feelings that come up when we're interacting with others and the world. Some of us are so protected by our programs that the idea of questioning them, even if we didn't know we were developing them, is just too frightening. I wonder what it is that causes our fear. What is this that scares us to the point that we're willing to continue to think or believe something, even if it's painful and unpleasant, instead of looking at it and questioning it? For some of us it's as simple as we have never thought to question what we think, and how we look at things. This isn't a choice known to us. Our programs are made up of set patterns of thoughts, feelings, and behaviors that haven't led us to challenge the truth about what we are seeing, feeling, or doing. You see, most patterns in a program continue to be used because they serve a purpose. They were, after all, developed for a reason; that's why we've kept them. We create patterns about how to get love and attention, how to protect ourselves, who to trust, and on and on. They then become so much of how we function that they become like habits, like automatic responses. It's when our programs don't seem to serve their purposes anymore that we begin to have to look for other ways. This can be a reason for change, but it doesn't necessarily mean that the program gets changed. Sometimes we just tweak the old program, trying to make it continue to fit or work, changing only some of the patterns. Sometimes we may just create another unhealthy program made up of faulty information from our other programs. Many of our programs and their patterns were formed to protect us emotionally from others. They may give us a false sense of high self-esteem because they help us to blame others for what we think, and how we feel. Remember my co-worker, Sue?

All people have faulty, mistaken programs. After all, most of society's messages don't teach us to look inside for answers; they teach us to blame outside things (the false myth discussed in PART ONE, Chapter II: Lasting,

Stable Happiness). Maybe they help to protect our self-esteem by helping us to think that we're superior to someone. Bottom line, we continue with the patterns in our programs because they help us in some way. Even if it seems to be an extreme type of pattern that causes more suffering, it has a purpose. It's when our self-esteem is threatened that fear usually arises because the strong protection patterns on our self-defense program have been alerted. Many of us would rather hold onto any belief or view that protects our self-esteem, even if it's unpleasant or causes us more suffering, than to look at what is behind our self-esteem being threatened. This is why the information in this book is so important. Once we begin to understand that our view of our self, our self-esteem, isn't based on anything except what we *choose to base it on*, then we can begin to let go of the protections we use. Only then can we let go of faulty, negative programs, and their patterns that cause us suffering, and begin to replace them with more healthy programs and patterns that increase our happiness. So how do we begin?

When I began my hospital chaplain education, there was an idea that the supervisor of the program introduced to us. This idea was that of FOOI: family of origin issues. Since this program saw self-awareness as very important, this idea was explained to help us see that we all come from the issues in our family and our experiences with these issues. The thought was that if we develop more awareness about these issues, we can use this awareness to help us get out of the way and be more there for our clients. It's thought that by gaining awareness into our prejudices, or our formed ways of thinking about certain issues or people, we will gain awareness into what work we need to do on ourselves so that we can help people in spite of our issues. I enjoyed this idea very much, because I have come to believe that, to put it simply, our faulty, mistaken programs from our FOOI are just that: phooey, untruths. If we are going to begin to understand ourselves, we must first begin with awareness: awareness of what our issues or patterns and programs are. We can then look at what is valid or true in our patterns, and what is simply phooey, untrue.

II

Beginning with Awareness

When I was working in the clinic at Kopan Monastery in Kathmandu, Nepal, there was an aggressive, Western, Buddhist nun who came to the monastery. She was quick to say what was on her mind, didn't seem to censor herself, and was often harsh with others. I chose to keep quiet when I had these unpleasant interactions with her. I remember thinking, "She's so lucky. If I wasn't practicing patience, I would eat her for breakfast." You see, in the past my pattern would have been to respond to this type of person with calm, polite, yet very cutting, matter-of-fact remarks about their behavior and their lack of taking responsibility for themselves. This pattern was my formed defense pattern that was often very cutting and powerful. I used this pattern in disagreements with my older sister when we were young. She would often end a disagreement with, "Excuse me for living." I would smile and say, "That's okay. It's not your fault." It was my way to keep my power and not give any to her.

Because I was practicing keeping quiet and watching what thoughts came up in my mind, I gained incredible awareness into the patterns in my self-defense program while interacting with this nun. At some point I even began to laugh at my crazy thought, "I would eat you for breakfast." In reality I'm grateful to her because, like her, I had been a type of person who had just thrown out my thoughts as if they were wisdom. I began to understand that in my previous work situations where I thought people liked me, in reality they were afraid of me. See how powerful keeping quiet, observing, and becoming aware can be? If I had come back at this woman I wouldn't have seen my patterns. I'm sure she wouldn't have responded to me in the same way anymore, but then I would have missed the opportunity for this powerful awareness about myself (we will talk more later about an outline for doing this work in difficult situations). I'm not telling you to not protect yourself in some way if you are in danger of physical harm. We can't do this work if we're dead. I'm talking about choosing to sit with and getting to know the patterns in the programs (software) on our mind (hard drive). This awareness is the key to one of the steps we will discuss later, the step of letting go.

> **LET'S STOP FOR A MINUTE. Let's think about this.**
> *Can you see the automatic thought-feeling program I developed when I was young to protect myself? I shared that I also used this program with my older sister. Do you think this program helped with my fear or reinforced my fear?* **Let's stop now and think. WHIGO?** *Look at my self-defense program;* **but** *what is yours? How do you defend yourself? Does this response help you or cause you suffering?*

If how we see things (our view) is clouded by what's already in place on our hard drive, and our beliefs about any situation are decided by our views, how do we begin to choose to see things differently? As cognitive therapy says, we must first begin to pay attention to what we are thinking and feeling. This goes back to the idea of, "What we resist, persists." If we don't pay attention to what's there, it's impossible to change it. *Awareness* is the key in the beginning. If we want to change how we feel, then we must change our thinking. Remember, our main goal is to increase our happiness and decrease our suffering.

As we start to pay attention to what we think and feel, we'll become aware of patterns. Sometimes they're easy to see, other times they aren't. If we open ourselves up to how others see us, this information can also be helpful. I'm not saying to believe everything that someone tells us about ourselves. Remember, they only know what we show them, and they see us through their programs. Others, though, can help us get clues about the more difficult, hard-to-see patterns. If we get the same response from more than one person, there may be some truth in it. If we're open to this information, then it's important to be sure that we get it from more than one person. We need to seek the view of many people. Then, don't judge it. We need to see it as information for us to look at. If we can go into this self-observation, self-awareness work without judging ourselves, it can be very powerful in starting to reduce our suffering.

It does seem to be part of our hard drives to judge what we see and hear. These judgements are from the makeup of our brains that takes the information coming in through our senses and then makes decisions about this information. Some of this information is true, like whether something is hot or cold; but many of these judgments come from our programs, such as deciding if something is good or bad. Just being aware of this can be very helpful. If we find ourselves judging what we see, find, or hear about ourselves, then this is also very important to see. Just how do we judge ourselves? What is this pattern? Keeping a journal to write down what we see can be very helpful. As we do this work, we'll find that our suffering decreases just by taking back our own personal power and understanding that we're more in control of our world than we thought. I have often heard people say they're scared to do this work because they're afraid of what they might find. This is when not judging ourselves is so important. Accepting where we're at helps us to know where to go next. Remember Secret Behavior number four: we're all doing the best we can for where we are at the time, we're all just doing what we think we need to do to be okay.

Remember, most of our patterns weren't put there by choice. They were created without our awareness. As we were growing and developing, most of them were put there by situations and experiences outside of our control, and by people in our lives who weren't aware they were helping us form certain patterns. Many others are a result of our child brain not correctly understanding the outside world because of our lack of mental, emotional, and physical maturity. As children, our minds aren't able to understand more complicated situations, so our ability to understand is limited. As children, we look to our parents as our role models and often copy their behavior.

Once I showed my ex-husband a picture of my mother. She was sitting with her elbow on a table, and she was touching two of her fingers together. My ex looked at me and said, "You do that." I asked him what he was talking about. He said I often put my fingers together like my mother was doing in the picture. I was totally surprised. I had no idea I did this. There was no reason that my mother would have taught me to do this. I believe this was just something I saw her doing, and I copied it.

> **LET'S STOP FOR A MINUTE. Let's think about this.**
> *I formed a behavior pattern from watching my mother. If I copied such a simple behavior of hers, what else must I have copied? I'm not aware that this behavior caused me any particular feelings. I wonder in what situations I did this behavior? Did it serve some purpose?* **Let's stop now and think. WHIGO?** *Think about how I copied this simple behavior;* **but** *what about you? What behaviors have you copied from your parents? Have they caused you happiness or suffering?*

A woman I know was talking to me about her four-year-old son. When I looked at his picture I saw a blond-haired, fair-skinned white boy. At one point she told me his father was black, and we talked about how surprising it was that he looked so white. She smiled and said, "Yeah, he tells me all the time that he wants to marry me, but he wants to look like his father." She then told me that her son had a stepsister from his father's side. His stepsister looked black. Her mother was white. This girl was always saying she wanted to look like her mother. These young children have parents of both races so there was no prejudice here. Each child wanted to look like the parent of the same sex, the parent who was the one they looked to so that they could understand what a boy or girl should be.

There were some thoughts, feelings, and behaviors that our parents and others around us tried to develop in us. These patterns are from what they thought was important, like being polite or saying thank you, or not talking to strangers. As we look at our patterns there may be feelings that come up about those who helped to create these programs in us. This is information for us and we can choose what we do with it. It's always important to remember, at all times, that we're all only human and have been and are doing the best that we can (Secret Behavior number four, we're all doing the best we can for where we are at the time; we're all just doing what we think we need to do to be okay). Unless we have done the work to be aware of our programs, we don't know that we're running on unknown programs. This doesn't mean we aren't responsible for our thoughts, feelings, and behavior; it only means we aren't aware that we're coming from programs that we didn't choose to create.

In the beginning when we are working on being more aware we're talking about using our awareness to watch our thoughts and feelings, and what's going on inside of us, just watching. As we become comfortable with watching ourselves, we'll become aware of patterns that occur. Sometimes it'll be easy to see thought-feeling patterns. Other times we may only be aware of the feelings that are part of an automatic thought-feeling pattern.

Some thoughts were learned so young that it might take the rest of our lives in therapy to become aware of them. If we start to watch what we feel, though, we can get an idea of the automatic thought-feeling patterns that we have in certain situations. Let's take the example we discussed earlier in Secret Behaviors number seven (No one can make us feel, think, say, or do anything) where someone calls us an unpleasant name. How do we respond to this? Maybe we immediately feel angry. If we pay attention to our inner response instead of reacting from the anger, then we can become aware of our thoughts and feelings that come up in this type of situation. We start with watching and becoming aware of what thought comes up after the situation happens. We then watch what feeling comes from that thought. We then continue with this watching: watching what thoughts and feelings continue to arise. If we follow all the thoughts and feelings that come up, we can start to get a clue that whenever someone responds to us in a way that we see as unpleasant, and maybe threatening, that our defense program goes off. Through this observation and awareness, we now have clues as to what our defense program may be. Is our defense program to feel angry? Are we even aware of what thought came up in us to create this feeling of anger? Can we begin to see how sometimes our programs have such strong automatic thought-feeling patterns that we aren't even aware of the thought that creates the feeling and that the feeling is the first thing we are aware of?

As we watch ourselves, we'll see that we'll have many thoughts and feelings in a situation until we move to the next step of choosing what action we'll take or how to behave. I recommend that as we begin to watch and become more aware of our thoughts and feelings, that at first we choose to do nothing but watch our programs. It's important to understand that we're in control of what goes on inside of us. It's also important, though, to understand that once we put something out into the world, we lose that control. We can't control what goes on outside of us or what happens once we put our thoughts and feelings outside to the world. This is why I'm saying that in the beginning, just watch what comes up, your responses. This watching can be very powerful in many ways. Seeing that we can be with our thoughts and feelings without reacting in some way is powerful in and of itself. It also gives us a great chance to increase our awareness of our patterned responses.

As I shared before, when my mother died I was angry with certain people whom I thought had been unkind to her. It took me years of therapy and self-searching to figure out the message I gave to myself about people at that time. I had always wondered about a contradiction I found in myself. From my awareness of my own suffering around my mother's death, I became very aware of others' suffering. What confused me was how I could be the most sensitive, kind, and loving person you could meet, but if I saw any type of threat I quickly became this cool, scorpion-tongued aggressor who had no problem going directly to the object of the threat and stinging them with my words. Having become aware of this contradiction at the end of my teens, I stopped voicing these attacks, but I began protecting myself through giving others an intense, heavy look of anger. One co-worker said to me once,

"Okay, I got it. Don't mess with me." So what was this inside of me that responded with such very strong defensiveness?

In therapy I found out that when my mother died, my eleven-year-old mind told itself, "If you let people walk on you, you will die." No wonder I responded so intensely when I saw any threat. By becoming aware of this program, I can now watch for it. People who have known me for some time now see me as being more gentle and "less angry" than I used to be. That's because now that I'm aware of this program, if it comes up I remind myself that this thinking comes from an untrue, child-minded pattern, and just let it go. We won't die from what other people say or do to us, because others don't have the power to harm us. Only we can make this happen by choosing to see what they do as harmful. Of course, this excludes physical harm.

> **LET'S STOP FOR A MINUTE. Let's think about this.** *Look at this automatic thought-feeling defense program I developed at such a young age. I changed from saying angry statements to giving people angry looks. Do you think this change was a change of the program or just a change in how I chose to display my self-protection program? Do you think this program helped me or caused me suffering?* **Let's stop now and think. WHIGO?** *Think about this program I developed as a child;* **but** *what about you? What automatic self-defense programs are you aware that you have? Are they helping you or causing you suffering?*

It's important to know that it's not necessary to do

this work alone. As we can see, I have had lots of help. When we're more comfortable with the work, we may choose to do it alone for different reasons, but it's not necessary to do it alone to be successful. Next, we'll talk about how to get help. We'll then talk about how to do the more in-depth work. We're going to talk about helpers first, because for some of us it can be very frightening to look at some of our old programs, especially if they're about some type of abuse. Again, it's important to understand that it's not necessary to do this work alone. There's nothing wrong with getting help. In fact, until we are used to and comfortable with doing this work, it's very helpful to have some support. This is especially true when we're dealing with very emotional thoughts and feelings like abuse. I know I'm grateful to those who have helped, and continue to help, me along the way. So I encourage everyone to look for helpers.

You see, we all need help at times; however, maybe "need" isn't true here. In reality, the only things we need to survive, no matter what we're feeling, are oxygen, food, water, and at times shelter. I don't want to help anyone create any new mistaken beliefs. It can be pleasant, though, to have others in our lives. It is mentally, emotionally, physically, and spiritually helpful to have others around us who help and support us. I want to stay in the reality that this is a choice, though, not a need. A need is something that must be present for us to continue to survive. Most people only need others in their lives when they're born; during that time, it is a need because we can't care for ourselves.

It's important to choose relationships that are helpful, not harmful. This isn't just when doing this work, but also in general. Our suffering won't decrease if we allow people in our lives who don't help us, who try to harm us in some way, or are unwilling to make an effort to be there for us. That doesn't mean that people with whom we have difficulty should be totally avoided. Sometimes avoiding them isn't possible or practical: for example, someone we work with. In these situations, we can choose to use them as a learning tool for ourselves. There is an interesting Buddhist way of thinking that the person who is upsetting us, or doing us some harm, is really our best friend. They say this because the person is giving us a chance to see how we think and feel and a chance to practice patience, compassion, and what they call equanimity. For example, The Dalai Lama of Tibet says that Mao Tse-tung, who was the Chinese leader who took over Tibet and killed many Tibetans, was one of his greatest teachers because he taught him patience. When we're first starting on a path, as we're talking about here, it's important to find supportive, mature helpers or supporters.

We may find a helper like a psychotherapist. We may choose to find our support in some spiritual path, whether that be a religion, some type of New Age group, or some type of personal growth, self-help group. Each of us must find our own particular path. As we look for what seems to be most helpful for us in this work, there are certain things to look for and certain things to avoid. If we find a teacher, therapist, or group of people we think might be helpful, it's important to observe them for some time. We don't want to do this work with anyone who is going to tell us what to think, how to feel, who we are, or what to believe, or who tries to control us with fear or guilt. If we run into such a person or group, it's best to *run away*. They will only help to create unhealthy feelings, insecurity, and confusion when we work with them. They will only help to create more unhelpful, often painful, software on our hard drives. They haven't done enough of the work themselves. We want help from someone who has done more of the work than we have. Observe their behavior. It's very important to trust our gut. When we leave them do we feel more strong somehow? Of course we can't be sure what's inside of them, but we can get clues from their behavior. Observe how much they seem to come from kindness and compassion. Watch to see if they're willing to look at and take responsibility for themselves. Observe how they deal with conflict and being challenged by others. Watch and see if they have respect for themselves and others. Remember, just because someone has a lot of clients, students, or followers, doesn't mean they will be helpful to you. They could be a wonderful person, far along on a path, or they could simply be great con artists who know how to take advantage of someone's weakness. We need to trust that part of us we call intuition, our instincts, or gut. If it doesn't feel right then avoid them, don't question it. It doesn't matter if we are right or wrong. What matters is that something inside of us says "not this person or group." *Listen.*

  Once I was invited to hear this "incredible," spiritual teacher speak. The woman who invited me told me, "You must come and see him. Anything that you want, he will get it for you." She meant whatever I wanted spiritually. I was suspicious about this because I didn't believe that anyone could get something spiritually for me. I decided to go, though, because this man's classes were very expensive, and this was a chance to hear him talk for free. All his words were very impressive. He seemed to be someone who was advanced in his own development. At the end he said he was going to do a "healing" meditation with us. As I closed my eyes to do this meditation I felt very uncomfortable. At first, I thought it was just me, brushed it off, and tried to let his healing meditation help me. This feeling of something unpleasant came again. I then stopped following his meditation. After the session, I talked to others, and they didn't have this feeling. Even though I couldn't find anyone else who felt this way, I decided not to attend this man's classes. Years later, I met a woman who knew this man, not as a teacher, but personally. She told me several stories about negative behavior he was involved with. I was glad I had listened to my instincts and kept my distance from this man. Whether this woman told the truth or not, didn't matter. What mattered was that I didn't feel comfortable with this person, and I listened to myself.

Some of us have heard stories about people who have been caught up in some type of cult. Things these groups usually do are to present their beliefs as the only correct way to think, encourage their members to avoid others who don't believe the same, and put down the beliefs of others. This type of group thinking is very important to avoid. The most famous cult leaders that many people know are Charles Manson and Jim Jones. They both isolated their followers from others to prevent them from being influenced by people who thought differently from them. A highly developed teacher will encourage us to look at all things, decide if *we* think what is talked about is valid and fits for us, and to not judge or put down the views and values of others.

A helper or support person is not someone who can do the work for us. I wish that was possible, but it isn't. That's why it's important to avoid people who say they can do the work for us, who tell us what to think and feel. A developed teacher or a knowledgeable therapist knows that they can only help us to find our own answers and to help ourselves. If we're looking for someone to tell us our answers and what to do, we're not ready for this work. This is okay. We're each wherever we are, and that is okay. As I said before, though, if we truly want to reduce our pain and suffering, which will mean we have to find *our* answers, then *we must begin to think for ourselves*. It will take some effort on our part to do this work. Even Buddha told his followers not to believe what he said just because he had said it. He said that we should check it out ourselves, and if we come to the same way of thinking, then okay. Remember, we all have our own specific minds, hardware with software. We can use similar ways to do the work but our specific mind will make our work specific to us.

Now we're going to begin to move into the next sections where we will begin to get into how to really do the work. It's important as we do this next work that we understand that the first and most important thing is to pay attention to what comes up in our minds, to become our own self-watcher. This is what we have just been talking about, the importance of awareness. As we begin to increase our awareness and begin to gain understanding of our patterns, we can find that this work can actually be fun; I did. It's like a mystery. As we watch what comes up it can be fun learning our specific patterns, our puzzle or mystery if we like. This is why some people find that keeping a journal is so helpful. It helps us to begin to see our thinking patterns, to gain awareness about ourselves.

The more we do this work the more we will become aware that there is a part of us that can be present and watching ourselves and others even as we talk and interact with others. I have heard it called the watcher. I'm not sure where I have heard this name, though. If we've ever been in an accident, robbed, assaulted, or involved in some type of frightening event, we've possibly seen this watcher part of us. I have heard people describe, and have experienced, this sense of watching things happen and how things slow down and are like a dream. This is the watcher watching with senses on high alert. I was working a job in a small village in India. One night the center where I was working was robbed. Twice that night I had guns pointed at me. Each time as I began to watch closely for a possible escape, I noticed how things became very slowed down, almost like a dream. This will not happen when we're doing our everyday watching, but in a threatening situation it can occur and is interesting to see. I'm using this example because a lot of people are aware of such stories and can understand the idea of a watcher. This watcher, though, is something we can tune into at any time or at all times. As I sit here typing, the watcher part of me is observing this.

III

Experiencing

The first step in this work is to watch and become aware, to become aware of our thoughts and feelings: *awareness*. This next step leads to letting go of, giving up, or deleting a program made up of certain thoughts and feelings. This is the step of letting ourselves think the thoughts and feel the feelings again. Sometimes we'll be aware of the thoughts and the feelings that come with them, other times only the feeling. It's important here, and this is where some people get frightened, to allow ourselves to feel whatever it is that we're feeling exactly at the time that it comes up. That means if we're watching a movie and we feel like crying, then go ahead and cry. It doesn't matter why. Each time we cry we're closer to becoming aware of something inside us. We need to just allow ourselves to feel and watch what else comes up. Does a past memory come up? Do we have pictures of something that happened in the past? Sometimes we will, sometimes we won't. Letting ourselves experience these feelings will help us begin to release and let go of them. There are times now that I will cry and I have no clue why; but "why" doesn't matter. If the feeling is there, I cry, or sometimes I just feel. We don't have to do anything but feel.

Expression of the feeling isn't necessary unless we want to move into letting go and releasing the emotion. If we do then there's one fewer memory, feeling, or thought being held in. As we discussed in the secrets list, we can't be rid of feelings or thoughts by hiding from them. We can only *begin* to be rid of them by re-experiencing them. The key to a lasting, stable happiness is letting go of unpleasant thoughts, feelings, and patterns that keep resurfacing to cause us suffering, cloud our view of our world, and prevent us from being happy. The key to beginning to delete, or get rid of, a program from our hard drive is re-experiencing the thoughts and feelings that make up the program. Now we may have heard computer experts say that once something is on the hard drive of our computer it can never be totally gone. Even if we delete it, there's still an imprint that can be raised. This is also true with us. The trick is to re-experience the feeling and then express it to such a point that we have released or let go of it. Once we have released the feeling connected with the thought, the thought no longer has power. It will go to the background as if it has been deleted. It can still be found in the back corners of our mind if desired. It just doesn't cause suffering anymore because it no longer has the powerful feelings connected to it. It's the feelings that are the center of the suffering. After all, even physical suffering is made stronger by feelings. If we experience the feeling and also change the thought that it was connected to, it is possible to not re-experience it again. If we've successfully changed our thinking and a situation occurs that brings up the old thoughts, they will quickly be replaced by the new ones.

One mistaken belief we should be aware of is thinking that we can be overwhelmed by our feelings, or that we don't have control over letting our feelings out once we start. This is totally not true. If we're letting ourselves feel something, and we start to become frightened, we can then think about something else and move away from the feeling. Remember that feelings come from thoughts. If we don't want to feel something, change the thoughts. This is a stress reduction method written about in many books. For example, if we're going to have surgery tomorrow, it really does us no good to dwell on the fear we may be feeling, so the suggestion is that we watch television or do something else to take our minds off our fear. I'm sure we've all done this before. Many of us seem to be pretty good at avoiding ourselves whether it's with computers, phones, music, television, or another activity.

As discussed before, I have heard many people express fear over "losing control." This is another mistaken belief that we hold to be true. This mistaken belief is the one that tells us if we express ourselves we'll lose control. If we believe this mistaken belief we also usually have the mistaken belief that by holding our feelings in, we will keep control. I tell people that the problem is not one of losing control but one of being "too controlled." It's like the pressure cooker or tea kettle example I talked about in Secret Behaviors number six (Resisting looking at ourselves will only increase our suffering, not make it go away). The pressure builds up from the repeated holding in of emotions, until it needs to be released. This is why some of us say that we feel we're going to lose control or blow up. There's no more room to hold in, or stuff, our feelings. The pressure has built up and needs to be released like the steam in a tea kettle. It's like we are full. With a pressure cooker or tea kettle, the pressure is released in the form of steam. If we're lucky our pressure is released in the healthy way that's built into our body for this purpose, tears.

The key here in this step is letting ourselves feel the feelings that we've been keeping inside, or any feelings that come up, that cause us pain and suffering. We can compare feelings to the save button on our computer. In order to save a thought program, there must be feelings that go with it. It's the feelings that give the power to the thought. Just think of all the different experiences and situations that are hard for us to remember. These are usually the experiences and situations that didn't mean much to us, where there wasn't much feeling connected to them. If there is a situation or experience, though, where we feel joy or hurt, these memories are much easier to recall. It's like the feeling is the save button. The stronger the feeling connected to a situation or experience, the easier it is to bring up the memories and thoughts about it. Of course there are situations where people have hidden memories because of heavy trauma. I'm not talking about these thoughts, although with support these memories can also be brought to the surface and examined. Usually in these situations, though, the person is aware of certain feelings. By letting the feelings come up, we reopen the program and can gain insight into the thought patterns on the program. We can then move to the next step and choose to not save the feelings again by expressing them in some way.

IV

Expression and Letting Go

The next step is expressing the feelings that we've re-experienced, to prevent us from holding them back in, and so that we can just let them go. In this step we're moving away from holding in towards letting go and giving up, or deleting, the thoughts and feelings that make up certain programs and their patterns. Usually we want to keep pleasant programs, so I'm not going to talk about deleting them. If we have a program with unpleasant feelings and we want to let go of this program, we must look for some way of expressing the feelings.

Let me say again that the body's built-in way for releasing the pressure from held-in emotions is crying. We've all experienced how hard and uncomfortable it can be to hold back tears. Tears can come up in both pleasant and unpleasant feeling situations. This is just an example of how tears are the body's built-in release and how resisting this release can feel uncomfortable. Tears aren't only the body's release valve, but are also the way to release the stress hormone, adrenocorticotropin. The release of this hormone then helps us to relax. So crying, or any form of the expression of a feeling, can be like the delete button. Each time we cry or express, we release the feeling. If we don't stop the feeling, holding it back in, then it's at least partly deleted. At least some of the pressure that goes with the feeling is released.

It's best to allow ourselves to express until we're done for that time. Until it's deleted, the feeling will come up again. Each time we allow ourselves to release and not hold back in, we're letting go of feelings. Eventually all the feelings that come with the thoughts (memories) that make-up a program can be expressed. After this the thoughts will seldom come up. It's then that it's helpful to look at changing the thoughts, if we are aware of them, so that we don't create new painful feelings. If we change the thought and the old thought comes up again, it will no longer cause any suffering. If unpleasant feelings come up again it means there's more expressing and letting go that needs to be done. It may just be on a different level or part of another pattern or program.

Sometimes we can release, and thereby let go, just by crying. Sometimes we may need to yell or scream. Sometimes we may need a helper. Helpers can help us to see things we can't because they're outside observers. There's no right or wrong unless we're hurting ourselves or someone else. This work doesn't require that we strike out at someone else or hurt ourselves in some way, which is a way of thinking that is just another mistaken, faulty, or unhealthy pattern. Just let what's there come out. That's all we have to do. Don't stop or judge it. If we do, it will continue, and we may just create more feelings that need releasing. Of course, I'm not talking about expressing our feelings about others with them. Here we are talking about *our* awareness work to help us gain understanding and release and let go. Expressing our feelings towards others is something we will discuss in later sections.

In 1993 I went alone into an eight-month retreat in Asia. Prior to this retreat, I still couldn't talk much about my mother's death without crying. If for no other reason than being alone and without any distractions like television, other people, and so on, I began to re-experience many of the old feelings that I hadn't let myself feel or experience for some time. Somehow, I knew to just let them flow. I did a lot of crying, sometimes sobbing, as I expressed all my held-in feelings around my mother's death. I also did this about an issue I have already discussed, the feeling of being totally alone. Since that retreat I have had no problem discussing anything around my mother's death. The held-in feelings have been let go. There were other feelings that I also let go, but this was the most powerful one. I also no longer have the fear about being totally alone. After all, I have myself.

> **LET'S STOP FOR A MINUTE. Let's think about this.** *What do you think my programs were that didn't let me express my feelings about my mother's death? Did these programs help me or cause me suffering?* **Stop now and think. WHIGO?** *Think about my programs; **but** what about you? What might be the programs that you have that stop you from re-experiencing old, held-in feelings? Are these programs helping you or causing you suffering?*

There are two mistaken beliefs about the expression of feelings. The first one seems to be a common, Western, mistaken belief about how the expression of certain feelings is a sign of weakness. Crying is seen as very weak. There are many sayings within Western cultures to stop us from crying. "Don't be a woos. Don't be a baby. Don't be a girl (for men). Don't be ..." This seems to be a stronger message for men, but women are also getting this message more now. Somehow this mistaken belief has taken root in certain societies. I have no clue why. This message doesn't seem to be part of many Asian cultures. In Asia I have seen men crying, often weeping, at the funeral of someone they love. This message doesn't seem to be the same for anger, though. Anger doesn't seem to be a sign of weakness, at least in Western cultures. There are cultures that see anger as a lack of self-development, a lack of maturity, or a type of weakness. What we're mainly talking about here is the feelings of fear, hurt, sadness, or any emotion which seems to show some type of vulnerability, or "weakness" in many people's minds. After all, anger doesn't show vulnerability. It's interesting, though, that anger is usually really about feeling hurt or afraid. It's just the fight instead of the flight reaction. *So*, is there any truth that showing or expressing these feelings is weakness, or does it show more strength to go against this mistaken belief and show or express these emotions? We all have them, so should we hide from experiencing and expressing this part of our humanness, these normal feelings?

There was a research study on the expression of feelings presented on a television news show. The two research subjects shown were one female and one male, approximately five years old. They hooked up monitors to the brain, heart, and skin of each child to measure their physical responses. They then showed each child the same video, but separately. This video had a lot of action-type scenes in it. We were first shown the little girl and watched as she jumped and moved about while watching these high-action scenes. We easily saw that she had a strong, unpleasant reaction. We were then shown the boy watching the same video. He sat cross-legged on the floor with his elbow resting on his leg and his chin resting on his hand. He sat quietly like this through the entire video and showed no reaction. The results on the physical brain, heart and skin monitors were the same for each child. The results were said to show how girls show their feelings outwardly or express them, and boys don't. The boy's mother said she didn't think she had given her son messages about not expressing his feelings, but that now she understood she had, unknowingly. This is an example of a thought-feeling pattern taught to a child which became a program about how to respond to the world. Seems there must have been some message he was taught about not showing how he feels. Can you see that the mother or possibly the father "unknowingly" taught this behavior to their child from one of their own programs?

> **LET'S STOP FOR A MINUTE. Let's think about this.** *How do you think this mother taught her son not to express his emotions? She wasn't aware that she did. Did he learn this from watching his father or mother or simply from their reactions when he showed his feelings? Do you think this program helped the child or caused him suffering?* **Let's stop now and think. WHIGO?** *Think about the programs this child developed;* **but** *what about you? What messages were you given about expressing*

your emotions? What programs were created in you about showing your feelings, especially crying? Have these programs helped you or caused you suffering?

It's interesting that we get taught and told not to cry, yet our body has this inner, built-in system for releasing built-up feelings and stress, called tears. The only other purpose of tears is to help to cleanse our eyes if there is something in them. Our body has this complicated system of ducts specifically designed for tears, and hormones specifically released when we cry. Is this some mistaken body design? Think about it. Seems illogical to me to deny the importance of this built-in stress reduction system.

In 1984 I was working as a psychotherapist at a community mental health center. While there I developed a six-session program called "Changing Patterns." This program was designed to help people who were thought of as chronically mentally ill. The program was about helping the clients look at how they thought, whether their thinking was true, and if they might want to start thinking differently. In the first session, clients filled out a questionnaire that was developed to look at what was going on in their lives at the time of their first admission to a psychiatric hospital. It was designed to see if there were any patterns that led to their hospitalization. I was quite surprised to see that the majority of these people had their first hospitalization after the loss of the most important person in their life. This person was different for each client from parents to partners, uncles, friends, and so on. These important people were the ones who had been there for them. The results of the questionnaire also showed that most of my clients had been the one in their family or group to express their feelings about this loss. Because this wasn't a formal research project, many people might question the results that I saw; but it seemed like most of my clients had been put into the hospital by their family or group after repeatedly expressing their grief by crying. This expression was not okay in their family or group. I saw this pattern repeat itself each time I restarted the group series. Overall, these patterns didn't surprise me, because I had already studied in theories of family therapy that the person called the "identified patient," or problem person in the family, is usually the healthiest person in the family. In these situations, the identified patient seemed to be the person healthy enough to express their feelings.

The second mistaken belief is about the idea that if we begin to express our feelings we won't be able to stop. We talked about this briefly in the experiencing section, but I want to stress that this is a mistaken belief. If this was a true belief, then we all would be caught up in our suffering feelings all the time. After all, we wouldn't have been able to stop them since they first happened. Think about it. If we weren't able to stop a feeling, then we would be caught up in that feeling all the time.

Now let's talk about letting go or giving up. I've often heard people talk about how hard it is to let go. Letting go begins with simply allowing whatever comes up to just be there. Then we don't do anything but feel and experience it, instead of stuffing it back in, which is what many people do from habit. Letting go isn't a separate step from re-experiencing thoughts and feelings and expressing them. Letting go *is* the expression and the not holding back in of the feelings. Letting go happens naturally when we don't hold something in or try to avoid it. If we just feel and express until we are finished for that time, we have let go automatically of whatever we just expressed. Letting go isn't this huge, difficult thing. It's the holding in that's the problem. People often say, "Well I just can't let go," of that thought, person, or memory. If we just let ourselves feel all the feelings connected with the thought, person, memory, situation, and so on and express them, we have let go. Of course, awareness and watching ourselves are very important in this work. The steps in this work aren't separate but build upon each other; they work together. If we aren't aware of something, we can't let it go. So, we first use awareness, then we allow ourselves to experience or re-experience. If we then express the feelings, or don't hold them back in, this is letting go.

If we're having trouble letting go of something, maybe there's some reason that we're choosing to not let it go. What is the thought pattern present at that time? What purpose does holding on to this pattern or situation serve? What are we getting out of holding on? This is why I use the terms letting go *or* "giving up." Are we willing to give up this pattern? This is a very important question that needs a lot of awareness. It may take time and repeated tries to let go before we gain an understanding of why we don't want to give up a pattern. This is okay. We never have to give it up if we don't want to. Remember, our main goal is a lasting, stable happiness. Is this pattern keeping us from being happy in some way? If yes, then we need to look at what we're getting from holding onto this pattern.

If we're continuing with letting go, we may need to

repeat the expression over and over for some time until we have gotten it all out. We will notice a spaciousness in our body after we have let go of something, especially if that something was a strong and painful memory or pattern. For me, and I have heard others describe it this way also, our body feels less heavy, lighter, and more spacious, and we have more energy. After all, we have just freed up the energy that we have been using to hold the feelings in.

We can't always know when we're done with expressing the feelings connected with a thought, memory, or program we want to delete. We have to continue to let ourselves just be, to feel and express. Expression can be through crying (best and healthiest choice, even if the first feeling is anger), yelling, writing down how we feel, throwing darts at the picture of someone who hurt us, going bowling and imagining the face of someone we don't like on the first pin, or hitting a pillow. There are no limits to the ways of expression. I suggest crying as the first choice. It's by far the most powerful and helpful way for letting go. The whole idea is to feel, and if we want to express at that time, to do something to put out the feeling. At some point we'll feel like the thought, memory, or pattern connected to the feeling no longer comes up and causes the same effect as it did before.

V

Changing Thoughts

We have reached the last step, how to change the thoughts that created the unpleasant feelings. The goal is to not create new unpleasant feelings from the old thought patterns. If we have already reduced the power of a thought pattern by letting go of the feelings that gave it power, we don't have to change the thoughts. It's best, though, to change the thoughts because of the many different thoughts and patterns in our programs that could create new unpleasant feelings. If we choose to do this work, we begin by changing the thoughts that we've become aware of. After all, it's not possible to change thoughts that we aren't aware of. Why would we want to change a thought? The main reason is that if the thought is faulty or mistaken, then it's helpful to replace it with thoughts that are true, give us strength, and are part of reality: thoughts that will helps us get the lasting happiness we want.

As a therapist I have often helped people look at three common types of thoughts that in reality are untrue, irrational thoughts. These are thoughts in which we blow situations out of proportion (catastrophizing), don't take responsibility for ourselves, and are being judgmental. We're talking about thoughts that aren't facts, which are instead mistaken beliefs that aren't based on reality, so they are called irrational.

Catastrophizing is making the situation bigger or worse than it is, blowing what did or might happen out of proportion. An example is when we say we're going to die if our girlfriend or boyfriend leaves us. Of course this isn't true or reality. We die from lack of oxygen, food, or water, some physical injury or disease, or, at times, exposure to the environment because of not having the shelter we need. We don't die from feelings. One might say, "Well what about dying from a broken heart? We hear this statement all the time." No one ever dies from a broken heart. This thinking just isn't true or part of reality. If we haven't done the work that we've been talking about, we will probably suffer when a relationship breaks up, or we lose someone close to us. It's possible, though, to feel differently because of what we tell ourselves about the situation. Catastrophizing thoughts create many feelings, but fear is the main one. When we're feeling fear, this often creates more fear and anxiety and can lead us to make unhealthy and irrational choices. It causes us to suffer in some way.

We have already spent a lot of time discussing not taking responsibility for our thoughts, feelings, and behavior. When we use words like "can't," "made me," or "should," we're not taking responsibility for ourselves. Most of the time these words keep us from admitting the truth or reality of a situation, which is that we're responsible for what we choose. When we take responsibility for ourselves we use words like "choose not to" or "don't want to." We can get clues about our thinking by watching what we say. It can be very powerful in changing the way we feel when we say "I don't choose to" or "I don't want to" instead of "can't," "made me," or "should." As we have already discussed, there is power in taking responsibility for ourselves. Blaming others, events or situations just creates a feeling of helplessness which strengthens the belief that we don't have control over ourselves, our lives, and the world around us. This blaming can also lead to fear or sometimes disguised fear: anger. These feelings don't lead us to make rational, healthy decisions. They cause suffering.

The "should" word is often connected to judgmental thinking. Who says we should? Should statements are often followed by guilt or shame feelings. It's a powerful thought pattern that can be broken when we understand what is behind our use of "should." "Who said we should?" Is there any truth to this thinking, or is it just another unaware, automatic thought, then feeling, pattern? Along with looking at our use of the word "should" with ourselves, it's also powerful to see how we use it to judge others. Remember, we only see others through our own programs, which clouds how we see them. Because of this they aren't responsible for our mistaken view of them. What program are we using to *should* someone? It isn't possible for us to develop high, positive self-esteem while we're full of guilt and shame. Let it go. It's not part of reality. It isn't true.

Let's talk directly about how we change the thoughts. We begin with paying attention, watching. Remember we can't change something if we aren't aware it's there. If we become aware of a thought that brings about unpleasant feelings, what do we do about it? The next step is to see if it has any truth in reality. Can we prove that this thinking is true, or is it created by a mistaken, automatic thought-feeling pattern? For example, say we are walking down the hall at work. We pass someone that we know and say hello. They don't speak back. Now how do we interpret their behavior? Do we think, "Well they're mad at me," and feel angry or hurt? Maybe we think they're being rude, and we feel angry. Maybe we feel hurt and think, "I don't care about them. I'll just stay away from them," which is a denial, defensive, protection pattern. Can you see how easy it is to respond to someone from our own patterns and mind? How do we really know how to understand why this person didn't speak to us? Do we have a true understanding on which to choose our reaction? No, we don't. We have no idea why this person acted like they did. So now we have choices. We can go with the automatic thoughts that came up for us and choose how to behave from one of our patterns, or we can do something different. We can decide that we don't have a true understanding on which to make a decision, and decide to do something about it.

The healthiest thing we can do is to simply talk to this person about what happened and ask them why they didn't speak to us. We may find that this person was upset about something and didn't even notice us in the hall. Have you ever been so deep in thought about something that you didn't notice something or someone? I know I have. Maybe this person has just gotten some bad news. Maybe we find out that this person doesn't want to give us an answer or responds in an unpleasant way. Even then, we can watch the thoughts and feelings that come up for us. If we're having thoughts that create unwanted or unpleasant feelings, the only way to change them is to replace them with true, reality thoughts that are more positive. After all, if this person doesn't like us, or responds to us in an unpleasant way, is there any truth to their thinking? Is there any reality in their thinking? Whigo? Well, the answer is no, unless we have told them everything that we think and feel inside, so that they then can make a more true, reality judgment. Even then, they can only see us from their own programs, so their judgments will be clouded. If they haven't reached completion, if completion is even possible, then there will be some kind of mistaken thought-feeling pattern from which they are seeing us. Remember, we aren't what other people judge us to be.

A friend of mine told me about a similar situation that happened to her. At Christmas time she gave a favorite type of cup to three of her friends at work. Two of these friends thanked her for the gift. The third woman didn't. My friend wondered for months why this third woman didn't mention the gift she had given to her. My friend then noticed that this woman had the cup she had given her at work. My friend said she was surprised that she had it at work and decided to ask her why she brought it to work. When my friend started talking with this woman she found out that the woman never got the present she gave her, and that this woman had gotten this cup on her own. My friend then discovered how she had set this cup aside and didn't realize that she had never given it to this woman. As they talked, they realized that they both had been feeling hurt for several months over a misunderstanding. The woman was hurt because she thought my friend had bought cups for the other two women and not her. My friend was hurt because she didn't think this woman valued her gift. So they were surprised to find out that they both were totally mistaken about what had happened. They were both able to then laugh about it.

> **LET'S STOP FOR A MINUTE. Let's think about this.** *We have two women who were upset and unhappy for months because of something they thought was true, but it wasn't. What do you think were their programs that stopped them from talking about this situation when it first happened?* **Let's stop now and think. WHIGO?** *Can you see that these two women suffered unnecessarily by not checking out what had happened between them?* **But** *what about you? Have you ever thought someone did something to you only to find out later that they didn't? Do you have some program that kept you from talking to someone when you were upset with them? Did this program help you or cause you suffering?*

Another good example to use to show how a thought pattern can be untrue is to look at when we say we "hate" a particular group of people. If we say we hate white people, Jewish people, black people, and so forth, we are showing a kind of thinking about very large groups of people. How can this type of thinking really be true if we haven't met all the people that make up the group? Aren't we really just deciding what to think because of thoughts that we have about a small number of people in this group? Maybe we've never even met someone belonging to this group. Maybe our thinking is only a mistaken thought-feeling pattern, a faulty software program put on our hard drive by someone else. It's very different to say we hate a certain person or people than to say we hate the entire ethnic, racial, or religious group that these people belong to. Does hate create pleasant feelings and help to increase our happiness? What is really behind the feeling of hate? What is this thought-feeling pattern?

One Christmas I was sitting outside a store in a very large, shopping mall with my ex-husband. While we sat there, a white woman walked by with a small, white boy who was probably about four years old. They continued walking, and I then heard this small boy yelling "Don't touch me nigger!" My ex and I were shocked as we saw that this boy had just walked by a black, adult man. Whether this man touched him or not, which was possible because the mall was very crowded, I don't know. All I know is that this small child yelled out those words.

> **LET'S STOP FOR A MINUTE. Let's think about this.** *What programs do you think this young boy has about black people? Are these programs he developed on his own? Are these programs helping him or causing him suffering?* **Let's stop now and think. WHIGO?** *Think about this boy's world view;* **but** *what about you? What are your programs about different people and things in the world? Did you choose these thoughts or were they learned somehow? Are these programs helping you or causing you suffering?*

I had several strong thoughts and feelings about this situation with the four-year-old white boy. First, how did this child know this negative term for a black person? Second, what has this child been taught that he would think it was okay to yell this negative term out loud at an adult? It's hard for me to imagine that this child learned this from his own experiences. He was just too young. It's more probable that this negative term and behavior are something he had been taught or had copied from the adults around him. I certainly didn't see his mother stop and discipline him. From my perspective, I consider teaching a child to hate as abusive. I say abusive because if nothing else hate doesn't create happy, pleasant feelings; instead, it creates negative, angry feelings. Hate interferes with their happiness.

We're never one thing or one way. We are a combination of thoughts and feelings. We can choose to act from whatever thoughts and feelings are coming up at a certain time or choose to do nothing but watch and examine what has come up. This is why it's important to understand that we can replace any thought with a thought that we decide is better, more true, more rational, or more in reality (we will talk in more detail about how to do this later in the outline presented on "aware, in-the-moment choices"). We can replace any automatic thought-feeling pattern with a number of more positive, true, reality thoughts which will create more pleasant or happy feelings. Now, it will take time to change an old thought pattern to a new one. Remember, if we want to change something, sometimes we must pretend to do it for some time in order to replace it and establish it as the new pattern. I'm going to share some examples from different schools of thought next so that we can get a clearer view of how to do this work, how to counter our thoughts with more helpful ways of thinking.

Virginia Satir (1916-1988) is someone I studied when I was working on my master's degree to become a psychotherapist. Her book *Peoplemaking*, now called *The New Peoplemaking*, was required reading because she is known as one of the pioneers in the field of family therapy. Her book is about how we develop our sense of self (self-esteem), especially as it's connected to our family. I have recommended this book to clients and friends over the years. In this book she has a poetic writing she calls *My Declaration of Self Esteem*, also known as *I Am Me*. I have shared this writing with many people over the years, and they have found it helpful. It talks directly about what I am explaining in this book. For this reason, I thought to share this writing with you.

<u>My Declaration of Self Esteem</u>
(also known as "I am me")

I am me.

In all the world, there is no one else exactly like me. There are persons who have some parts like me, but no one adds up exactly like me. Therefore, everything that comes out of me is authentically mine because I alone chose it.

I own everything about me: my body, including everything it does; my mind, including all its thoughts and ideas; my eyes, including the images of all they behold; my feelings, whatever they may be: anger, joy, frustration, love, disappointment, excitement; my mouth, and all the words that come out of it: polite, sweet or rough, correct or incorrect; my voice, loud or soft; and all my actions, whether they be to others or to myself.

I own my fantasies, my dreams, my hopes, my fears.

I own all my triumphs and successes, all my failures and mistakes.

Because I own all of me, I can become intimately acquainted with me. By so doing, I can love me and be friendly with me in all my parts. I can then make it possible for all of me to work in my best interests.

I know there are aspects about myself that puzzle me, and other aspects that I do not know. But as long as I am friendly and loving to myself, I can courageously and hopefully look for the solutions to the puzzles and for ways to find out more about me.

However I look and sound, whatever I say and do, and whatever I think and feel at a given moment in time is me. This is authentic and represents where I am at that moment in time.

When I review later how I looked and sounded, what I said and did, and how I thought and felt, some parts may turn out to be unfitting. I can discard that which is unfitting, and keep that which proved fitting, and invent something new for that which I discarded.

I can see, hear, feel, think, say, and do. I have the tools to survive, to be close to others, to be productive, and to make sense and order out of the world of people and things outside of me.

I own me, and therefore, I can engineer me.

I am me and I am okay.

Satir 1988.

(Permission to print from The Virginia Satir Global Network on 01/28/2016)

Most religions have some type of prayer or teaching that shares their wisdom about how to change the way we think; in other words, what to replace our negative thinking with. Religious teachings often have the message of changing our mind by helping or caring for others. Remember when we discussed earlier that the Dalai Lama said that if we are going to be selfish to be wise selfish. This thinking is about helping and caring for others because it helps us. This can be a very powerful and rewarding way to counter our thoughts. Even this method isn't really helpful, though, if we are using it to stuff down and avoid looking at, knowing, and experiencing our own feelings. If we use these teachings to hide from ourselves, they just become another way of avoiding ourselves and will prevent a lasting, stable happiness. These are very good methods to use as we are doing the work and pretending to think and thereby, feel a certain way. They're powerful methods for replacing negative thinking.

I have had several Christians tell me that they have found *The Prayer of St. Francis of Assisi* (Appendix II) to be helpful. In my studies of Buddhism, I have had several teachings on a prayer called *The Eight Verses of Thought Transformation* by Geshe Langri Tangpa (Appendix III). If we look at this prayer, we'll see that Buddhists have some very specific ideas about what to replace negative thoughts with. I found this prayer very helpful in working to change my thinking. We can't behave according to these lovely prayers unless we're aware. We must pay attention in order to follow this advice. The bottom line with using any method is to pay attention and not just reboot our computer brain and act on its probably faulty, mistaken, software programs. Stop, pay attention and if needed, replace the thought with a different thought. Over time and with practice, we can become good at this method.

There is a writing that was found on the wall in Mother Teresa's home for children in Calcutta, India. It's thought to have been written by her, but because it wasn't signed no one can be certain that it was. I wanted to share these incredible thoughts here.

Do It Anyway

People are often unreasonable, irrational, and self-centered. Forgive them anyway.

If you are kind, people may accuse you of selfish, ulterior motives. Be kind anyway.

If you are successful, you will win some unfaithful friends and some genuine enemies. Succeed anyway.

If you are honest and sincere, people may deceive you. Be honest and sincere anyway.

What you spend years creating, others could destroy overnight. Create anyway.

If you find serenity and happiness, some may be jealous. Be happy anyway.

The good you do today, will often be forgotten. Do good anyway.

Give the best you have, and it will never be enough. Give your best anyway.

In the final analysis, it is between you and God. It was never between you and them anyway.

Whether we believe in God or not, maybe we can see the wisdom in this writing. When I read this, my thought was that it's not between us and them, it's between us and ourselves, the software on our hard drive against our true nature. We're only affected by others and events if we *choose* to be so.

Let's pull these ideas all together. How do we find and keep happiness? Happiness is connected with feeling good. We can begin to feel more pleasant feelings just by starting to become aware of ourselves, our thoughts and feelings. If we then continue on this path of experiencing, expression and letting go, and changing the faulty, mistaken thoughts in our programs, our happiness will become more and more stable, and it will last. This isn't quick or something we can do overnight. It's an ongoing, continuing effort. We can do as little or as much as we want and take as long as we want or need. I promise, though, that our happiness will increase with self-awareness. The key to happiness is looking inside and coming to know and understand ourselves. If we choose this path, we're entering into a life of becoming a more inner being. By this I mean we are paying attention to what is inside of us and are looking there for the answers.

What about this common belief that we can find happiness in possessions, in possessing people and objects? The problem with this belief is that if we look outside ourselves for answers, then our happiness will always depend on things that we can't control. We can't control others, so they may leave or abuse us. All physical objects break down with time. Our new car will never be brand new again. It will age each day and need repairs. The same goes for our young, gorgeous mate. Remember how we talked about people who are rich and famous, who we think have everything, who are still unhappy? We even hear of these people committing suicide. Why would Kurt Cobain, the lead singer for the music group Nirvana, kill himself? He had good looks, wealth, fame, a pretty wife, a child. What else do we need? If we don't have an inner life the world can seem very boring, empty, and crazy.

When we start to go inside and develop an inner life we get an extra bonus. We start to get in touch with that part of us that's called our spirit or soul. Getting in touch with our spirit or soul can really make our life amazing and special. Once we look to ourselves for our happiness, our happiness no longer depends on things outside of us, and it won't go up and down as it did before. Our happiness will become more stable. The ups and downs will depend on our ability to see our mistaken patterns and to stop or change the thoughts and feelings that make them up. This is how we keep our happiness. We're in control, not others. If we look for happiness on the outside we'll go back and forth between feeling happy and unhappy, or hurt, very quickly. That's because we're looking to the outside world to decide how we feel. If we look inside, we can understand that only we have the control over how we feel. We can create our own world and that can be a world with lasting, stable happiness.

In the next section we're going to discuss an outline that we can put in place for making rational, aware, in-the-moment choices for acting in different situations. If we use this outline, we can keep our happiness overall. Until we've reached completion, though, if that is really even possible, we'll have some ups and downs. This can just be more information about more and deeper thoughts, feelings, and patterns to be released. With each release we'll just find more inner spaciousness, peace, and happiness. The inner path decreases the frequency and degree of the ups and downs, and our thoughts and feelings become more stable. We move from, "What the hell is going on?" to Whigo?

This inner life is also the key to learning to love ourselves and to become our own best friends. When we learn to love ourselves, we'll no longer make choices that cause us any type of pain or suffering. It's actually self-abuse when we choose a behavior that we know will have unpleasant results. Remember, we can only control what *we* think, feel, and do, and not others. We can choose how we behave, but we can't choose the results of our choices. I have often told clients that they will only hear me preach one thing: that's to make choices that help us, not choices that harm us. We may not be able to control the results, but very often we're aware that certain choices may bring about positive or negative results. The only possible way to affect the results is to be aware of what the results for different choices might be. This can't always be known, though, because of things outside of us that are out of our control.

Being an inner person just means experiencing and being aware of what's going on inside of us. It's very helpful to take our inner awareness to another level of working to understand our thoughts and feelings. We can easily look inside just by lying on our couch and thinking. Think about how we felt about our day. It can be even more effective to sit up with our legs crossed, in what is called the meditation position, and just watch what comes up in our mind. If something is troubling us, just think about what it is and then watch the feelings that come up. As we watch our feelings and the other thoughts that arise, we can often get answers to any questions we might have. Being quiet and with ourselves is the key to gaining more understanding about the patterns we have inside. It is another book, though, for me to get into discussing the way of choosing to take this path even deeper. We don't have to choose to do this. Simply by becoming aware of our inner thoughts and feelings, we will decrease our suffering.

VI

An Outline for Aware, In-The-Moment Choices

Let's look at an outline for dealing with different situations that come up. We can use this simple outline with any situation, from someone dying, our boss yelling at us, or the alarm clock not going off. When a situation arises:

1) Tell yourself to *STOP* (or you can say whigo if you have learned to use it to stop automatic patterns). We can say stop out loud to ourselves if we need to. Saying stop will help to stop the habitual, automatic thought-feeling pattern that may be arising.

2) Stop whatever it is that you are doing and just begin to pay attention to your inner self.

3) Begin to watch your thoughts and feelings. Don't do anything else, just watch. Remember, we don't have to choose to do anything else.

*If the situation is something that doesn't involve an interaction with someone else, go on to the eighth step. If people are involved, continue with step four.

4) Now, pay attention to the behavior of the other person with whom you are or have been interacting.

Remember these secrets/truths:

A) They are also human like us, so they experience pain and suffering.

B) They want to be happy and loved like us. They are just trying to make themselves okay in some way.

C) They are operating from their specific programs, just like us.

D) If they appear or state they are unhappy, this is a choice they have made.

E) We are not responsible for what someone else thinks or feels or how they choose to behave.

F) No matter what they are or have been doing or saying, they are not responsible for our reactions to them.

G) If someone is reacting in an unpleasant way, they are suffering for some reason. One of their negative programs has gone off and they are reacting from it.

H) MOST IMPORTANT, *remember that if they are blaming us in some way that they don't know what is inside of us, so they can't make a true or correct judgment about us for that reason. The same is true about our judgments of them.*

*Hopefully, remembering these ideas will keep us from falling into one of our negative, automatic thought-feeling patterns, like we may have done in the past.

5) As we watch this other person, remember again that we all have pain and suffering. If this person is upset, then they are re-experiencing some pain and suffering at that time. Remember that we all react to situations from our thought-feeling patterns.

6) Remember again that this person only knows what we show them, so anything they say about us is a faulty, mistaken belief from *their* thought-feeling patterns.

7) Once we are reminded of the other person's pain and suffering, it's time to remember that if a person is not showing kindness or patience that this behavior could be a sign of insecurity. Is their self-esteem being threatened? Are they wearing a mask?

8) The purpose of all these steps is to remind ourselves that there is no need to be threatened by anything that happens. We can watch the thoughts and feelings that come up, but are they true and from reality? We don't have to go along with them. The only way someone or something can hurt us is physically. We are in control of whether we feel hurt or upset emotionally or mentally. We decide how to see or understand the situation. If a person isn't involved, it's easier because we only have to deal with the mistaken beliefs of our own mind, not theirs, too.

9) Now that we've reminded ourselves of these things, we can decide how we want to choose to behave. If we feel that we're in a good place and can express ourselves well and in an assertive way, then we can go ahead and express ourselves. Assertive behavior involves using the word "I" to take responsibility for what we're going to say and then

using a verb like feel, believe, or think. Remember we aren't being assertive if we're yelling, crying, or blaming the other person for how we think or feel. We're acting out of some automatic pattern. This isn't bad. These thoughts and feelings can be good for gaining understanding about our patterns; *but,* gaining understanding isn't the goal at this time. This is why it's good to take some time to respond to certain situations. We may need to work through the thought-feeling pattern that has come up that makes us take the situation personally. After all, if we aren't responsible for others' thoughts and feelings, if they aren't responsible for our thoughts and feelings, and because we're both viewing each other from our own mistaken patterns, then how can either of our thoughts and feelings really be personal? They or we may try to make it personal, but this isn't reality because we have no truth on which to make our judgments.

If we don't believe we can express ourselves in a positive, assertive way, then sometimes it's better to choose to keep quiet, take some time, and then discuss the situation with the person later. I'm not saying to put on a mask and pretend that what's happened doesn't bother us in some way. I'm simply saying that choosing to remain quiet and not respond in certain situations, usually where either person has strong feelings, is a way to keep our power by not reacting to the other person's behavior. If needed, we can simply excuse ourselves or tell the other person that we "choose" not to continue with or to discuss the matter further. If they try to continue the interaction, then we can again choose to remove ourselves from the situation. Of course we can choose to go ahead and respond, but if we're acting out of a thought-feeling pattern that we don't have much understanding about, then we might not like the results that happen from this unaware response.

The point here is that we choose how we're going to see or understand anything that we experience. We can react from an old, possibly untrue, program pattern or we can do something different. Remember, and as many times as it takes, that the other person isn't responsible for our thoughts, feelings, and behavior, even if they're in our face screaming at us. I'm not saying to allow others to abuse us. I'm just talking about what's happening inside. If we tune into the pain and suffering that the other person must be experiencing, especially in an unpleasant interaction, then we can greatly reduce our own unpleasant feelings and be less threatened by a situation.

If another person isn't involved, then we simply look at our thoughts that are coming up and how they make us feel. Remember, if we want to change how we feel we must change how we think. If the alarm clock didn't go off, is it really something to get upset about? What are we telling ourselves about what happened? Are we worried about the reaction of our boss, our co-workers, or a client? If we're upset, it's connected with how we see things and our judgments about the event. Are we exaggerating (catastrophizing) about the possible results? If we aren't, it's important to remember that no matter what happens, we'll survive. Even if we lose our job, don't have money for food, or don't have a place to stay, there are always choices. It isn't a pleasant outcome in the minds of most of us, but there are many homeless people surviving. What's the worst thing that could happen? Most would say the worst thing that could happen is we die. Remember, we die first from lack of oxygen, then from lack of water, then from lack of food, and last from lack of shelter if the weather is extreme. If we're in a Western country there are usually places to find help with food and shelter, and clean water is easily found and free. So if we deal with what's the worst thing that could happen, then the more minor results won't even affect us.

If the situation involves something more traumatic, like the loss of someone close to us, then the path is the same. Pay attention to the thoughts and feelings coming up. Don't judge them. Expect that you will go through the stages of grief, and at times this feels a bit crazy. You can still use this outline and the ideas in this book. When you tune into your feelings are you blowing things out of proportion, judging yourself or someone else, or "should-ing" yourself? Often when we lose someone close to us we go through a phase of wondering what we *should have done* differently with them. This is shoulding yourself. I should have done this or that. The past is the past, it will never come again, and we're all very smart when we look at the past to decide what we *should* have done. That's because in the current moment we know things that we didn't know in the past. If you decide you wish you had done something differently with a person, whether they are alive or not, this can be used to decide how you want to change your thoughts and behaviors in the future. Awareness is the key. Avoiding your thoughts and feelings will only increase your suffering and really serves no purpose. Avoiding just doesn't help you in any way. Remember the importance of expressing and letting go.

SOME ANSWERS An Outline for Aware, In-the-Moment Choices

10) After the situation is over, take the time to look inside and go over what happened during the situation. How were you feeling? What was your thinking? Did there seem to be a true connection between what happened in the situation and the thoughts and feelings that came up, or did the thoughts and feelings seem to come from an automatic, thought-feeling program on your hard drive (mind)? Do you want to choose to react differently next time?

VII

WHIGO

How do we begin to use the acronym whigo (pronounced whig-oe) to replace the question, "What the hell is going on?" Once we get better at doing this inner work, or maybe from the beginning if it works for us, instead of saying stop when the thoughts are coming up, try saying "whigo." Try saying the word whigo again. How do we feel when we say this word? Whigo seems to be the type of word that when said, from its very nature, makes it difficult to feel anger or confusion. It's a more lighthearted sounding and feeling word. Try using this word when a situation comes up instead of stop. Of course, we use whigo as we would use the word stop, to stop our thoughts or to stop ourselves from going into an automatic pattern. We say it in our mind or out loud if it's more helpful. See if this helps to stop some of the unpleasant feelings that come up.

If we set up this word in our mind as something that can make us smile, then when a situation comes up and we say whigo we'll be able to smile, at least inside. It can help to steer us away from a negative pattern. After all, if a situation comes up and we immediately feel like smiling with whigo, we'll be in a much better place to deal more positively inwardly and outwardly with any situation. We should try to establish the pattern of having whigo come up whenever we feel anything unpleasant. It can then help to get us to laugh at ourselves, others, and the wild world that we live in. After all, because we all come from our specific programs, we're all a bit delusional about what we see, a bit crazy, but not in a negative way. I find that smiling and laughing at my wild mind, and what comes up in it, greatly increases the experience of joy that I have when interacting with the world. Of course, as with all of us, some days this is easier than other days. Whigo is just another fun word I have begun to use to replace anything negative that comes up in my mind. Be careful though. Be careful to not use the word whigo as a way of not looking at and understanding our negative programs. Still do the work in the outline.

Let's pull these ideas all together briefly. We now have several ways to increase our happiness. Just by becoming aware of what is going on inside of us, our thoughts and feelings, our happiness will increase. This is especially true if we're taking responsibility for our thoughts and feelings, and thereby taking back control of our lives. If we decide to continue on the path and begin to re-experience our feelings, we'll not only gain insight into our programs but reduce the suffering that comes with stuffing in emotions. If we then continue on with expression and letting go, our happiness deepens, we free up energy, and we'll find our suffering is reduced. If we choose to look at the thoughts that aren't part of reality and cause unpleasant feelings to come up, and then replace them with true, reality thoughts, this will send the old program thoughts to the back of our mind, deleting them to some extent. Our happiness will then become much more stable. The key to any of these methods is being aware of what is going on inside of us, which is the real key to happiness. Remember, what we resist, persists; or in other words, it's impossible to change or deal with anything that we aren't aware of. Remember, **we create our own world.** *Remember,* no matter what we do, we need to be kind to ourselves and take our time. This is what will really make the work beneficial and helpful.

· PART FOUR ·

ENDING WITH THE QUESTION

Ending with "THE QUESTION"

Now that we've talked about the question, our secrets, and some answers, what's our answer now to the question, "What the hell is going on?" Well, the first and most true answer is, *always*, "us." We're all going on at all times in our own, specific way. The brain never stops even during sleep; our thoughts are just in the form of dreams during sleep. If we're asking the question about someone else, the first true answer is us and then them. The world we live in is the constant interaction between peoples' inner selves, our programs. Those who don't know or understand the secrets and answers talked about here, continue to look outside of themselves for the answers and for happiness, a solution which, more often than not, causes them suffering. They won't find a lasting, stable happiness this way.

 As I end this book, I want to share the answers I found to four of the questions that I had on my journey. I talked about these questions previously in the introduction chapter. I want to be specific about the answers I found to "What the hell is going on?" First, "Why do people go out of their way to hurt other people?" Bottom line, if someone is trying to hurt others, this behavior comes from their mistaken belief that they can somehow feel better about themselves by hurting others. I have found that people who do this have low self-esteem. Because of their low self-esteem, they're either so caught up in their own suffering that they don't think to be aware of others, or because of their mistaken beliefs, they're wanting others to feel as bad as they feel, thinking it will help them feel better somehow. I've often heard people say, "I wanted them to feel like I feel," when they're talking about having hurt someone. Of course, this isn't possible in reality; it's not really possible for someone to "feel like I feel." For whatever reason, it doesn't work for any period of time. We can't be successful, in the long run, in feeling better about ourselves by hurting others. This is a mistaken, irrational belief with no truth in reality. In fact, the result of this type of behavior is usually the opposite of feeling better about ourselves: an even lower self-esteem.

Remember Kathy, my neighbor friend who was unkind to me the night before and day that my mother died? Kathy's mother was very abusive to her. Before my mother died I was at her home several times and witnessed her mother yelling at her, calling her names, and grabbing and hitting her with a thin, wooden, ping pong type paddle. As a small child I was horrified by seeing my friend beaten. When I was older, another of our friends told me that she once saw Kathy's mother kick her down the stairs. How did this small child named Kathy feel when these events happened? She certainly got plenty of messages that she was bad. I believe these experiences are why Kathy went out of her way to hurt others. I think her self-esteem was very low. It's sad to know that she continued this behavior into adulthood.

Second, "What do we do with the anger that comes up when we feel threatened?" My first response is to say do nothing but watch what's there; then, if we choose, we can try to understand where the anger is coming from. If we then choose to react in some way, it will be an aware choice not an automatic program response. Of course, if we've read this book we can understand that the whole idea, the thought or feeling of being threatened, is faulty, mistaken thinking most of the time. Unless someone is directly, obviously threatening us physically, it's likely that there isn't even a true reason for feeling threatened. If there's a true reason, then of course we must protect ourselves. If not, then the anger isn't necessary. Anger is just the fight reaction to fear, and if there's no true reason for fear, then there's no true reason for anger. So first do nothing but pay attention, observe. This is the simple, yet powerful and profound, answer I found in the Buddhist beliefs I studied. In the West we seem to think we must *do* something to react. It can take a minute to actually understand, though, that just watching and being aware *is* doing something.

Third, "Is basic human suffering different from culture to culture?" I would say that all human beings experience similar suffering. I would like to say that we experience the same suffering, but this isn't true because we each experience suffering in our specific way. There is a difference also in what each culture says is important. What our culture says is important, what it tells us we should try to obtain to be happy and so on, is what we will put out effort to obtain. Otherwise, human suffering is not different from one culture to another. We all suffer from the secrets discussed in this book. We all share this condition of being human.

Fourth, "If everyone around us is suffering from this basic human condition, how do we really help people decrease their suffering? What is the bottom line here?" To me, the bottom line is to help people understand two things. We must understand that we're not alone in our suffering, we're all in this human condition together. Just understanding this can reduce our thoughts of being alone and isolated. If we take this understanding, along with the understanding that a lasting happiness can only be found from an inner path, then our feelings of isolation and lacking control, or helplessness, can stop. The key to decreasing our suffering is to be more and more aware of and understand ourselves, to become an inner being, and to take total responsibility for ourselves. Understanding these things is very powerful in helping us to get the lasting, stable happiness we all want.

A friend of mine said that she thought inner peace was a luxury for those with more money and not something for people who don't have so much, for instance those who are poor. In other words, do people who lack the way to easily meet their basic needs have less inner peace? As I thought about this, I remembered that the most peaceful people I've met have been Buddhist monks who have given up the desire for outer things and taken a total inward path. We talked about Maslow's hierarchy of needs. He does say that we must meet our basic needs of food, water, and shelter before we can move through the other levels to reach self-actualization, our full potential for happiness. I think, though, that in the Western cultures we increase our mental and emotional suffering because we have more time to pay attention to and create unhappiness in our minds. In more poor countries, where people are worried about meeting their basic needs of food, water, and shelter, they seem to spend less time thinking about happiness or unhappiness. Remember the story I told you about people I met in India telling me they'd "never thought about" whether they were happy? Some of the more peaceful people I have met in India were poor villagers. Our economic status doesn't have to interfere with us having an inner life. Some of my Indian friends may still be more concerned about the basics of food and water, but because some have taken an inner path, they do seem happy, even if they don't think about whether they are. In fact, there's an interesting Buddhist teaching about the suffering that comes from having a lot and all the energy and worry that goes with trying to keep these things. I know that I became more happy when I simplified my life.

I had a teacher when I was in graduate school who said everything has to do with power and sex. I told her I didn't believe that. I agree that these are obvious issues that seem to be talked about frequently in our world. I say, though, that everything has to do with our level of self-esteem, how we feel about ourselves. Our whole world is a constant attempt to feel good, to be happy. How we feel about ourselves affects all. Our self- esteem is one of the main filters through which we view our world. Power with or over others is just an outside way to try to deal with our insecurities, our low self-esteem, and the helplessness that we feel from not taking responsibility for and control of our own lives. What does sex have to do with our self-esteem? Well, if we're too afraid to connect with someone emotionally and in a healthy way, for some people the physical act of sex is a non-threatening, pleasurable way to connect with someone and feel good. It's still trying to feel good. Actually, it's an outside way to try to feel good whether we can or can't connect with the other person. I wanted to just briefly touch on the ideas of power and sex, two outside ways to try to feel better and happy. Because power and sex are very common, frequent, outside ways that people use to try to feel good, to find happiness, I thought they needed to be talked about briefly.

The bottom line is that a life of inner awareness and taking responsibility for ourselves is what greatly increases our happiness, *not* the outside attempts, which always depend on things we can't control. The belief that we can find a lasting happiness from things outside of ourselves is a common, mistaken belief that we all seem to be taught. Often this mistaken belief is taught just from the lack of understanding that this belief is mistaken. It's the false myth that pervades many societies. For those who do know better, it seems no one really stands up and says loudly that this belief is not true, that this belief is a mistaken way to believe. I'm trying to stand up now and let this truth be known. I hope everyone can hear.

In PART ONE, Chapter II: Lasting, Stable Happiness, I talked about the false myth, the mistaken belief that we're taught by our societies about how to find happiness. This myth is about how we can find happiness through things outside of ourselves, through finding the right person, making a lot of money, accomplishing certain things and the list goes on and on. To summarize the points we discussed about the false myth, they are:

Most societies encourage the false myth, a mistaken

belief, that a lasting happiness can be found from things outside of ourselves.

This mistaken belief is an idealized, exaggerated reality.

This outer search creates unhappiness and suffering in us.

This outside search encourages the false belief that things outside of us, people, events, and so forth, are responsible for our feelings, thoughts, and behavior.

This blaming of outside things for what we think, feel, or do, which has no truth in reality, leads to a feeling of helplessness that prevents the development of self-confidence and a high, positive self-esteem.

With these beliefs in mind, I had several goals for writing this book. First, I wanted to openly shout out loud that *it is not true that we can find a lasting, stable happiness outside of ourselves, with outside things.* By letting it be known that this common, daily reinforced belief isn't true, my hope was and is to help us to become aware of a rational, true path for finding a lasting, stable happiness. If we want a lasting, stable happiness we must take the inner path. This is the only rational, true, reality path that will give us the high self-esteem and confidence we need to attain a lasting, stable happiness. This is why I'm trying to make known the mistaken and false beliefs that cause us to be so unhappy. They only cause a feeling of helplessness and confusion.

Second, I wanted everyone to become aware of what we all share as human beings. I wanted to move these experiences from being secret to being known. By making these secrets known, my goal was to help reduce our sense of being alone and isolated in our human experience. This feeling of sharing our similar human experiences hopefully has and will continue to help to increase our self-esteem. After all, why feel less about ourselves when we're all in the same boat? *Believing we're alone in our experiences is just a false mistaken belief.*

Overall, I have two goals. First, to reduce our sense of being alone and isolated to thereby strengthen our sense of belonging; and second, to reduce our sense of helplessness and lack of control by strengthening us with the reality that we're in control of our inner world and our inner reactions with the world outside of us. The idea is to set up the true, rational belief that we're not at the mercy of anything outside of us, that we really do create our own world. This is why I have presented a case for making these false beliefs known. The ultimate goal is to help reduce our suffering by allowing us to develop the inner strength, confidence, and high self-esteem that come from taking responsibility for ourselves. The taking of responsibility for our thoughts, feelings, and behavior is the key to reducing the feeling of helplessness that comes with the path of an outside search for happiness. Understanding that a lasting, stable happiness and inner strength can only be found through an inner search or inner path, is essential for getting the lasting happiness and confidence we seek.

When I teach, and after conducting therapy sessions, I often end with reminding people to be kind to themselves. I have learned that it's important to say what I mean by being kind to ourselves. If we're making choices that cause us pain and suffering, I consider this self-abuse. Being kind to ourselves doesn't mean, for example, that if we're overweight, we should let ourselves eat those cookies we want. Actually, being kind to ourselves means making the choice that's going to help us the most. Sometimes that means sacrifice or work. It may mean not eating those cookies. It may mean getting up early to exercise or meditate. It may mean keeping silent and working with our thoughts and feelings when someone is attacking us verbally. Being kind to ourselves most certainly means making the choice to take an inner path that will bring an end to our lack of self-confidence, helplessness, and confusion. A lasting, stable happiness is just the reward!

There's a book that came out called *Eat, Pray, Love* by Elizabeth Gilbert. I know many people read and enjoyed this book. A woman I worked with when this book was released enjoyed it, but said to me, "But who has months to take off and run around on a spiritual trip?" I'm saying here that this isn't necessary. We can start right now where we're sitting or standing just by stopping and paying attention to what we're thinking and feeling. Often we're so busy with life's routines that we're not aware of what we're thinking or feeling. We can still be busy going about our day *and* still be paying attention to what we're thinking and feeling. We must strengthen the watcher in us and make it our friend, our best friend and constant companion. We'll then come to know our thoughts and feelings and be more happy.

Let me caution you about something, though: this work isn't about being insecure about what we're thinking and feeling. It isn't about being quiet so we don't say or do the wrong thing. This work is about becoming aware of ourselves, how we think about what's going on outside of us, and becoming more happy and secure through self-awareness and the power of being in control of our reactions to the world. Please don't use this work as a way to doubt yourself. If we do this, we've missed the point and are still looking outside of ourselves to be okay.

Can we imagine what the world would be like if each and every person in the world examined our minds and programs, took responsibility for ourselves, and no longer tried to increase our self-esteem from outside of ourselves and, at times, at the expense of others? I can, and I pray for this. After all, why would there be a reason for war and greed if we each stopped blaming others for our situations, thoughts, and feelings and found our power from within.

There was a young man I worked with who was talking to me about his father. He said he is "so much softer" than his father. We then began to talk about how his father had been an adult in Bosnia during the Balkan War. We talked about how difficult it must have been for him to fight in this war and how it probably affected how he is. I then began to talk about this idea of how we're programed. We talked about how men and women are born with their hard drives, which includes the hormones that help the body to function and can affect our feelings, and how everything else outside of our hard drive is the result of software programs. We're all human beings first. The programs we're taught about how a woman or man should be are just that, *taught*. Men and women are not different other than the hard drives they are born with and the things they are taught about how or who to be. Being human is the one thing we all share. We talked about how sad it was that his father was taught to hold in his feelings and how this has seemed to make him "hard." In reality it is more likely that this behavior is his father's attempt to hold in all kinds of traumatic feelings that must have arisen when he fought in the war. **The bottom line is**, we are all human beings first; putting the hormones aside, men and woman aren't so different, simply because *we are all human beings first.*

I know that most of us aren't giving up our lives to go meditate in some isolated place. The point I'm making in this book is that we don't have to do this, that just by stopping the outer search for and dependence upon outer things for happiness, we can begin and advance on a path to a greater lasting, stable happiness. Albert Ellis stated in the introduction to his book *A Guide to Rational Living* that "... humans tell themselves various sane and crazy things. Their beliefs, attitudes, opinions and philosophies often take the form of internalized sentences or self-talk. Consequently, they can change their self-defeating emotions and behaviors, by their clearly seeing, disputing and acting against their internal philosophies" (Ellis and Harper 1997). If the power each of us wanted was found within our own personal power, there would be no reason for war because we would know and understand our own personal power, instead of trying to have it with or over others or trying to get more things, thinking that possessions will make us feel better about ourselves. We would have gained the power we seek and understand that there is no need to look outside or elsewhere for it.

I think it's expressed well in the music lyrics of the song *Imagine* by the wise man named John Lennon. Lennon sings about everyone sharing the world, living in peace, and living in the moment. Lennon expressed his hope that we and the world could all join together (Lennon 1971). *I choose to be a dreamer, like Lennon writes about, and I am grateful I am not alone on this path. I hope that you will take an inner path, so that your world will be full of joy and peace.* This is my dream and my motivation for writing this book. I can and will choose to continue to imagine while I'm in this life that we are all free of suffering. I thank you for reading this book and ask you to please be kind to yourself.

· APPENDICES ·

APPENDIX I

An Outline for Aware, In-The-Moment Choices
(Synopsis)

1) Tell yourself to stop or say whigo.

2) Pay attention to your inner self.

3) Observe your thoughts and feelings

If another person is not involved go to number 8.

4) Pay attention to the behavior of the other person.

   Remember these secrets/truths about others:

   A) They are human like you.

   B) They are trying to make themselves okay.

   C) They are operating from their specific programs, just like you.

   D) If they are unhappy this is a choice.

   E) You are not responsible for what they think, feel, or do.

   F) They are not responsible for your reactions.

   G) If they are reacting in a negative way they are suffering.

H) MOST IMPORTANT, remember that if they are blaming you in some way, that they don't know what is inside of you and can't make a true or correct judgment about you for that reason. The same is true about your judgments of them.

5) Remember, we all have pain and suffering. If they are upset, then they are definitely re-experiencing a thought-feeling pattern.

6) Remember, this person only knows what you show them.

7) Remember that, if a person is not displaying kindness or patience, this behavior could be a sign of insecurity or low self-esteem.

8) Remind yourself that there is no need to be threatened by anything that happens.

9) Decide how you want to choose to behave.

10) After the situation is over, take the time for more inner awareness.

APPENDIX II

The Prayer of Saint Francis of Assisi

Lord, make me an instrument of your peace.
Where there is hatred, let me sow love,
Where there is injury, pardon,
Where there is doubt, faith,
Where there is despair, hope,
Where there is darkness, light,
And where there is sadness, joy.

O Divine Master, grant that I may not so much seek to be consoled as to console,
To be understood as to understand,
To be loved as to love,
For it is in giving that we receive,
It is in pardoning that we are pardoned,
And it is in dying that we are born to eternal life. Amen.

APPENDIX III

The Eight Verses of Thought Transformation
by Geshe Langri Tangpa (1054-1123)

Determined to obtain the greatest possible benefit for all sentient beings, who are more precious than a wish-fulfilling gem, I shall hold them most dear at all times.

When in the company of others, I shall consider myself as the lowest of all and from the depths of my heart hold others dear and supreme.

Vigilant, the moment a delusion appears in my mind, endangering myself and others, I shall confront and avert it without delay.

Whenever I see beings that are wicked in nature and overwhelmed by violent negative actions and suffering, I shall hold such rare ones dear as if I had found a precious treasure.

When out of envy others treat me with abuse, insults or the like, I shall accept defeat and offer the victory to others.

When someone whom I have benefited and in whom I have great hopes, gives me terrible harm, I shall regard that person as my holy guru.

In short, both directly and indirectly, I offer every happiness and benefit to all my mothers. I shall secretly take upon myself all their harmful actions and suffering.

Undefiled by the stains of the superstitions of the eight worldly concerns, by perceiving all phenomena as illusory, may I be released from the bondage of suffering.

REFERENCES

Assisi, St. Francis of. The Prayer of St. Francis of Assisi. Retrieved from http://www.Catholic-forum.com/saints/pray0027.htm.

Dray, Kaleigh. (2012, Feb 19) Kevin Costner's Moving Eulogy for Whitney Houston. *entertain wise.* Retrieved from http://www.entertainwise.com/news/ 69961/-Kevin-Costner-Moving-Eulogy-For-Whitney-Houston.

Ellis, Albert and Harper, Robert A. (1997) *A Guide to Rational Living.* (3rd ed.). Chatsworth, CA: Wilshire Book Company.

Keys, Alicia. (2011) The Life. *metrolyrics. Beyond the words.* Retrieved from http://www.metrolyrics.com/the-life-lyrics-alicia-keys.

Lama, His Holiness the Dalai. (1981) Commentary on the Eight Verses of Thought Transformation by Geshe Langri Tangpa. *Lama Yeshe Wisdom Archives, The Archive of FPMT.* Retrieved from http://www.lamayeshe.com/hhdl/8verses.html.

Lennon, John. (1971) Imagine. *metrolyrics. Beyond the words.* Retrieved from http://www.metrolyrics.com/imagine-lyrics-john-lennon.

Maslow, A.H. (1943) A Theory of Human Motivation. *Psychological Review,* vol. 50(4), Jul 1943, 370-396.

Satir, Virginia (1988) *THE NEW PEOPLEMAKING.* Mountain View, California: Science and Behavior Books, Inc.

Self-Actualization. *Merriam-Webster Dictionary.* Retrieved from http://www.merriam-webster.com/dictionary/selfactualization.

Simons, Janet A., Irwin, Donald B. and Drinnien, Beverly A. (1987). Maslow's Hierarchy of Needs. *Psychology-The Search for Understanding.* Retrieved from http://honolulu.hawaii.edu/itranet/committees/FacDevCom/guidebk/teachtip/maslow.htm.

Teresa, Mother. Do It Anyway. *The Prayer Foundation.* Retrieved from http://www.prayerfoundation.org/mother_teresa_do_it_anywayhtm.

www.ingramcontent.com/pod-product-compliance
Lightning Source LLC
Chambersburg PA
CBHW021144080526
44588CB00008B/203

* 9 7 8 1 9 4 2 5 4 5 5 3 8 *